LANGUAGE WORKS

9

English Literacy Resource

Robert Cutting

LanguageWorks 9 Workbook

Cutting, Robert, 1952–
  LanguageWorks 9 workbook

(Prentice Hall language)
Supplement to: ResourceLines 9/10/Robert Dawe, Barry Duncan, Wendy Mathieu.
ISBN 0-13-026286-2

1. English language – Problems, exercises, etc. – Juvenile literature.
2. English language – Grammar – Problems, exercises, etc. – Juvenile literature.
I. Dawe, Robert T. (Robert Thomas), 1948– . ResourceLines 9/10. II. Title. III. Series.

PE1112.D297 1999 Suppl.   428   C00-931658-2

Prentice-Hall, Inc., Upper Saddle River, New Jersey
Prentice-Hall International, Inc., London
Prentice-Hall of Australia, Pty., Ltd., Sydney
Prentice-Hall of India Pvt., New Delhi
Prentice-Hall of Japan, Inc., Tokyo
Prentice-Hall of Southeast Asia (PTE) Ltd., Singapore
Editora Prentice-Hall do Brasil Ltda., Rio de Janeiro
Prentice-Hall Hispanoamericana, S.A., Mexico

ISBN 0-13-026280-3

Director of Secondary Publishing: Paula Goepfert
Publisher: Mark Cobham
Project Manager: Sara Jane Kennerley
Editorial Consultant: Robin Pearson
Contributing Writer: Anthony Luengo
Production Editors: Laurel Bishop, Kendra McKnight
Research Editor: Linda Sheppard
Production Co-ordinator: Sandra Magill
Cover/Interior Design: Alex Li
Cover photographs: Digital imagery® copyright 1999 PhotoDisc, Inc.

Printed and bound in Canada
1 2 3 4 5 WC 04 03 02 01 00

LANGUAGE*WORKS* 9

TABLE OF CONTENTS

Unit 3 Grammar and Usage **45**

Unit 4 Putting It Together! **81**

Unit 5 Review and Reference 107

Unit 6 Preparing for Tests in Reading and Writing   133

WELCOME TO LANGUAGE*WORKS*

Welcome to **LanguageWorks 9**! This workbook will increase your understanding of the English language and will help develop your writing skills. It is made up of the following six units:

- Vocabulary
- Spelling, Capitalization, Punctuation
- Grammar and Usage
- Putting It Together!
- Review and Reference
- Preparing for Tests in Reading and Writing

Each unit begins with a **Focus On** page. This is similar to a *pretest* on the contents of the lessons that follow. At the end of each unit, there are **Check Up** pages that evaluate how much you have learned. Extra help is given in the **Review** pages in unit five. Unit six will help you prepare for the Reading and Writing Tests in Grade 10.

Whether you follow each lesson, one page to the next, or concentrate on the lessons that will help you the most, **LanguageWorks 9** will be a valuable resource during your first year in Secondary school!

Unit 1

Vocabulary

FOCUS ON: Vocabulary

Use the activities on this page to check up on your **vocabulary** skills.

1. For each word, identify any **prefix, suffix,** and the **root word**.

    (a) semifinal: _____

    (b) happiness: _____

    (c) disagreeable: _____

    (d) reproducible: _____

    (e) retroactive: _____

2. Check the correct answer.

    Synonyms are: __ opposite in meaning __ words that are spelled the same

    __ different words with similar meanings __ words that sound the same

3. Check the correct answer.

    Antonyms are: __ opposite in meaning __ words that are spelled the same

    __ different words with similar meanings __ words that sound the same

4. Circle the word pairs that are **homonyms**.

right left	**cymbal symbol**	**in into**
today yesterday	**hire higher**	**tract tracked**

5. **Similes** use _____ or _____ when comparing ideas.

6. Here is an example of a **metaphor:**

    The **sea was a raging beast** in the storm.

    Write a **metaphor** to finish this sentence beginning.

    The wind _____

7. Here is an example of **personification:**

    The **windows watched** the crowd as it walked by.

    Write an example of **personification** to finish this sentence beginning.

    The chair _____

Vocabulary

The **root form** (or base form) of a word is the form of the word without any affixes.

un + **happy** + ly = unhappily   **agree** + ment = agreement
(root form)   (root form)

> When affixes are added to root forms, the spelling can often change.

> Root forms change their meanings as affixes are added.

1. Identify the **root forms** in these words.

   flying: _____   underrated: _____

   problematic: _____   cloudy: _____

   declassify: _____   disinterested: _____

2. Add **affixes** to these root forms to make at least two new words for each root form.

   music: _____

   load: _____

   fall: _____

   real: _____

   machine: _____

   correct: _____

   day: _____

3. Add **affixes** to these root forms. Use each affixed root in one or more sentences.

   create: _____

   _____

   fumble: _____

   _____

   team: _____

   _____

   back: _____

   _____

Describe your classroom or tell about something you will see on your way home today. Write a short passage in your journal using only the root forms of words.

Vocabulary

Look at the meanings of these **prefixes**:

> e.g. hyperactive: more active

> A **prefix** will change the meaning of a root form.

hyper- : more than usual; more

hypo- : less than usual; under

mis- : wrong or bad

extra- : beyond; outside the scope of

pre- : before or at an earlier time

retro- : backward; back

pro- : for or in favour of

out- : greater, better, or separate place

1. Write **meanings** for these prefixed words. Use the prefix meanings as a guide. Check your meanings in a dictionary.

   hypersensitive: _____

   hypocentre: _____

   misinform: _____

   extraordinary:_____

   retrofit: _____

   pro-labour: _____

   outrun: _____

   > Some prefixes use a hyphen (-) when attaching to a word.

2. (a) Write at least two **prefixed words** for each of these prefixes.

   under- : _____

   in- : _____

   over- : _____

   anti- : _____

   mid- : _____

   tri- : _____

   (b) Use at least five of your **prefixed words** in a short paragraph that shows their meanings.

   _____

   _____

   _____

   _____

   _____

 Research other prefixes. Make a list of them, keeping the prefixes with you as you write stories.

 **Vocabulary** *Suffixes*

Look at the meanings of these **suffixes**:

-able, -ible: capable of ——————

> e.g. perishable: capable of perishing or rotting

-ate: provide with ——————

> A **suffix** will change the meaning of a root form.

-less: lack of; without

-ful: full of; character of

-ment: result of; condition of

-like: similar to

-wise: with respect to

-ward, -wards: in the direction of

1. Write **meanings** for these suffixed words. Use the suffix meanings as a guide. Check your meanings in a dictionary.

   reproducible: _____

   refrigerate: _____

   helpless: _____

   tearful: _____

   amazement: _____

   lifelike: _____

   lengthwise: _____

   backward: _____

2. (a) Write at least two **suffixed words** for each of these suffixes.

   -est: _____

   -ship: _____

   -tion: _____

   -hood: _____

   -ish: _____

   (b) Use at least five of your **suffixed words** in a short paragraph that shows their meanings.

   _____

   _____

   _____

 Research other suffixes. Make a list of them, to keep with you when you write stories.

Vocabulary

Synonyms can be used when you want equivalent, but more suitable words in your writing.

I **said** I was innocent.

I **claimed** I was innocent.

> **Synonyms** are different words with similar meanings.

(**Claimed**, a synonym of **said**, is a more suitable choice for the meaning given.)

1. Add at least three more **synonyms** for each of these words.

   > A thesaurus is an excellent source of synonyms.

   industry: <u>commerce,</u> _____

   first: <u>earliest,</u> _____

   proceed: <u>begin,</u> _____

   stress: <u>burden,</u> _____

   dishonest: <u>corrupt,</u> _____

   blanket: <u>covering,</u> _____

2. Rewrite each sentence using **synonyms** from Activity #1 to replace the **boldfaced** words.

   (a) We shall **proceed** to set up our **industry** at the **first** opportunity.

   _____

   (b) Don't **blanket** a **dishonest** act; it will only **stress** you.

   _____

3. Write three sentences that use **synonyms** of these words:

   mix   **pleasant**   **truth**   **dreary**

   _____

   _____

   _____

   _____

   _____

   _____

   _____

   _____

 Select a piece of writing, such as a song lyric you like. Rewrite it using synonyms of some of the words. Did the meaning of the piece change?

 **Vocabulary**

Antonyms can add to the meaning of an idea by using opposite thoughts.

We **started** the season as champions, but **finished** out of the playoffs.

> **Antonyms** are words opposite in meaning.

Your **positive** comments outweigh the **negative** feelings of the team.

1. Use **antonyms** of the **boldfaced** words to add to their meanings and complete these sentences.

   (a) We **quickly** boarded the airplane, _____

   _____

   (b) The story had a **foolish** beginning, _____

   _____

   (c) We must **succeed** where others have tried, _____

   _____

   (d) In the **quiet** of her home, _____

   _____

   (e) You may be **smart**, _____

   _____

2. Write sentences using these **antonym pairs**.

   merciless—merciful: _____

   _____

   smile—frown: _____

   _____

3. Rewrite this paragraph using **antonyms** to give the opposite meaning.

   I was satisfied with my pay. It was the most my employer would give me. With it, I can buy almost anything I want.

   _____

   _____

 Write an advertisement based on a well-known product, using antonyms to give the opposite meaning.

Vocabulary

Look at how these **homonyms** have different meanings:

There were many **sales** on **sails** last month.

I knew that a **new gnu** was born at the zoo yesterday.

> **Homonyms** are words that sound the same, may be spelled the same, but have different meanings.

> Make sure you use the correct homonym in context.

1. Complete these definitions with **homonym pairs**.

   (a) molecular biological material; pants: genes, _____

   (b) moved through the air; a viral sickness: _____, _____

   (c) money; odorous: _____, _____

   (d) a number; completed eating: _____, _____

   (e) one who foretells; monetary gain: _____, _____

   (f) a spice; measuring the passage of this: _____, _____

2. Use each of these **homonym pairs** in a sentence.

   weak—week: _____

   _____

   sundae—Sunday: _____

   _____

   lessen—lesson: _____

   _____

3. Give a **homonym** for each of these words, then use the word pairs in a paragraph.

   cereal—_____   **boarder**—_____

   guest—_____   **side**—_____

   _____

   _____

   _____

   _____

   _____

   _____

   _____

   _____

   _____

▶▶ *Write some homonym triplets:* to—too—two. **How many can you think of?**

Vocabulary

Everyday speech often includes **slang** and **jargon**. In most cases, slang is very local, and expressions used in one city or country can be very different from those of another place. It's also quickly dated: what was slang many years ago may have little meaning today.

> **Slang** expressions are "coined" or created to describe something in a colloquial or common way.

1. Match these older **slang expressions** with their actual meanings.

down to Earth	realistic
a crumb	a mental hospital
pip-squeak	unkind name for a person
the loony-bin	one who is insignificant

   > These slang expressions come from the early 1900s.

   Which of the four slang expressions do you hear being used today?

   _____

   What meanings do they have today?

   _____

   _____

   _____

2. Write down a **slang expression** used today. Give its meaning, then use it in a sentence to show its meaning.

   > Although slang and obscenities often are used interchangeably, look for a slang term that doesn't use swear words.

   _____

   _____

   _____

3. Here's a sentence using **computer jargon**. Underline the computer jargon words.

   > **Jargon** can be the language used for a specialized or technical area, such as computers.

   We attached a cable modem, then a scanner onto the bus port before downloading four megs of data onto the zip drive.

   Write a sentence using **jargon** from a specialized field (such as a sport or a type of work) that you know.

   _____

   _____

   _____

▶▶ *Make a list of slang terms that seem obsolete now.*

9

Vocabulary

Dialect and Colloquialism

Read this example of automobile dialect:

I pushed the fuel performance to its upper limit by changing the PCV valve and re-gapping the spark plugs.

> A **dialect** can be the language that is particular to a group (i.e., automobile dialect), or similar to jargon.

Now, read the same example only written in a colloquial way.

You know, I tweaked this gas guzzler by throwing in a new PCV valve and tightening the plug gaps.

> **Colloquial** language is informal in nature, suited more to oral usage.

1. Rewrite these **colloquial sentences** using **dialectal language** suitable to the theme words in **boldface**.

    (a) **maps:** Well, take yourself down aways on Merton Street about two blocks toward the sunset, and you'll get there.

    _____

    _____

    (b) **television:** I just sat in front of the tube, surfed the channels, and found this great bit on skateboarding.

    _____

    _____

2. Write a sentence in the **dialect** of one of these themes:

    fashion   **music**   **sports**

    _____

    _____

    _____

    Now, rewrite your sentence in a **colloquial** way.

    _____

    _____

    _____

    _____

    _____

    _____

 Find examples of dialectal and colloquial language in everyday sources, such as newspapers. Gather these and share them with classmates.

 **Vocabulary** *Standard English*

This sentence uses **standard English** in giving a direction:

Pour the liquid carefully from the test tube into the 500-ml beaker.

This sentence uses **standard English** in giving a description:

The lake shimmered with the beauty of the sun as a gentle breeze caused miniature ripples on the water's surface.

> **Standard English** is formal language, free of jargon, slang, or colloquialisms. It is most often used in formal speech and writing. A standard dialect would use the formal words particular to a certain dialect. Standard Canadian English dialect uses words that may not be present in other English dialects: **pemmican, pingo, nor'wester, tundra**, for example.

This dialogue uses **standard English**:

"I hope that you are successful," said the Captain.

"My mission will not be in vain," replied the Ensign.

Use **standard English** to write one of the following:

- a set of directions for a recipe, sport, or programming a VCR

- a description of a city scene, a crowd scene, or a dream

- a dialogue between two friends, an employer and an employee, or a coach and a player

Write at least three sentences on the subject you chose. You may wish to put your writing in paragraph form.

_____

_____

_____

_____

_____

_____

_____

_____

_____

_____

 Search for examples of standard English in everyday sources, such as magazines. Gather these and share them with your classmates.

Vocabulary

When should you use **formal** language? When is **informal** language acceptable? Use the ideas on this page to help you decide.

> **Formal language** is standard English. **Informal language** is colloquial.

1. Make a list of when you feel **formal language** should be used.

   _____

   _____

   _____

   _____

2. Make a list of when you feel **informal language** is acceptable.

   _____

   _____

   _____

   _____

3. Write **formal** or **informal** for each of these, indicating the type of language you feel is needed.

   filling out a prescription: _____

   waiting in line for a movie: _____

   explaining what's wrong with a computer: _____

   thinking about your future: _____

   making a new dinner dish: _____

   explaining a play to the rest of the team: _____

   asking for a raise in pay: _____

   explaining why your homework is incomplete: _____

4. Select one of the situations in Activity #3. Write a short paragraph about it, using the type of language you suggested.

   _____

   _____

   _____

   _____

   _____

▶▶ *Which is easier for you to use: formal or informal language? Respond to this formally or informally.*

Vocabulary

Similes can make descriptions more vivid. Examine how similes improve this sentence:

Jaleen ran fast in the race.

Jaleen ran **as fast as a cheetah** in the race.

Jaleen ran **like a cheetah** in the race.

(The similes **as fast as a cheetah** and **like a cheetah** give the reader a more vivid sense of how fast Jaleen ran.)

> **Similes** are descriptions that use **like** or **as**, such as **ran as fast as a cheetah**, or **like a cheetah**. They compare two unlike things, such as Jaleen and a cheetah.

> For example:
> • flying like an eagle
> • flying as high as a kite

1. Create two **similes** for each of these ideas: use **like** in one simile, and **as** in the other.

   (a) jumping: _____

   _____

   (b) thinking: _____

   _____

   (c) climbing: _____

   _____

   (d) sat: _____

   _____

   (e) fell: _____

   _____

2. Rewrite these sentences. Add **similes** to improve them.

   (a) Marcus told stories about the old country.

   _____

   _____

   (b) Karen shops at the local mall.

   _____

   _____

3. Write your own sentences for these ideas. Use **similes** to add description.

   (a) riding a dirt bike: _____

   _____

   (b) cramming for a test: _____

   _____

▶▶ *Listen to people as they talk. Make a note of when they use similes in their speech.*

Vocabulary

Metaphors also add to a piece of writing by making descriptions more vivid. Consider how a metaphor improves this sentence.

The crowd moved toward the building.

The crowd **swarmed** the building.

(The metaphor here gives a more exact description of **how** the crowd moved toward the building.)

> A **metaphor** is a direct comparison between two things. The **literal** or actual meaning of one thing is applied to the other: "The crowd **swarmed** the building." implies that the crowd moved like a large group of bees.

1. These sentences use **metaphors**. Write what you think each one means.

   (a) His mind was **a desolate place**.

   _____

   (b) The car **leaped past** the rest of the racers.

   _____

   (c) "We **towered** over their team by the end of the game!" exclaimed the coach.

   _____

2. Complete these sentence fragments with **metaphors**.

   (a) The party was _____

   (b) My vacation _____

   (c) Studying for the exam _____

3. Write a short (four or five sentences) paragraph on one of these topics. Use **metaphors** where possible to add description.

   buying a computer   **first alien contact**

   acting a part on stage   **being lost in a forest**

   _____

   _____

   _____

   _____

   _____

   _____

   _____

 Rewrite a popular song lyric indicating what metaphors are used and including additional metaphors.

Vocabulary

Personification makes a piece of writing more vivid by adding descriptions with human appeal. Consider how personification improves this sentence.

> **Personification** is the giving of human characteristics to non-human things and inanimate objects: e.g. The old ship **ached and moaned** as it moved through the waves.

The old ship moved through the waves.

The old ship **ached and moaned** as it moved through the waves.

(The personification here suggests that the old ship made sounds as if it were in pain.)

1. Improve these sentences with **personification**. Add human characteristics to make the idea more descriptive.

   > For example: The wind **howled** around the crowd.

   (a) The water _____ at us in our boat.

   (b) The clouds _____ the airplane as it flew through.

   (c) Rain _____ as we ran for cover.

2. Select one of the following subjects. Write a list of **personifying ideas** that could be used to describe your choice.

   > For example: **rock**: tripping; screaming through the air; punching the ground

   dog   tree   table   carpet   wind   car   water   pen   computer   TV

   _____

   _____

   _____

3. Create a single-frame cartoon using **personification**. Use ideas from Activity #2. Put the object in a situation that shows its human characteristics as real.

   > For example: a rock drawn as it is actually screaming

 Extend your idea in Activity #3 into a multi-panel comic strip featuring personification.

Vocabulary

Borrowed Words

The English language has always borrowed words from other languages. Eventually, these words are used so often, that they **become** a part of English.

Our language is rich in vocabulary from other cultures. Look at these examples: **barbecue** (Haitian); **guru** (Hindi); **canoe** (First Nations); **eureka** (Greek). Each word is instantly recognized as part of English.

1. Try to match these **borrowed words** with their origin languages in the box. (HINT: Check your guesses in a dictionary.)

    Arabic   Hungarian   Japanese   Algonkian   Italian   Scandinavian

    saga:_____   coach: _____

    magazine: _____   pilot:_____

    hickory:_____   tycoon: _____

2. Here are some **borrowed words**. Write a brief meaning of each, then give its country of origin. You may want to use a dictionary for this.

    Dictionaries mention words' country of origin

    shampoo: _____

    banana: _____

    tundra: _____

    chef:_____

    pretzel: _____

3. Use the clues to guess what the **borrowed words** are.

    (a) This Dutch word describes a salad side dish made with shredded cabbage. _____

    (b) This Polynesian word describes a design or picture imbedded in the skin. _____

    (c) This Persian word describes a type of sweater worn over the shoulders. _____

4. Here are some **borrowed phrases**. Write what you think each phrase means.

    à la carte: _____

    faux pas: _____

    alter ego: _____

    status quo: _____

    Use one of the phrases in a sentence to show its meaning.

    _____

    _____

    _____

 Select a word from another language. Use it in everyday speech. See if it becomes acceptable.

 # Vocabulary

Etymology is the study of the origin of words. Many of our words trace their history to ancient Roman and Greek times.

> The etymology of a word can tell how its meaning came into English and changed over the years.

flexible: from the Latin (Roman) word **flex** meaning "to bend"

autograph: from two Greek words **auto** (self) and **graph** (something that writes or is written)

1. Use these Latin and Greek words to make recognizable modern words. Use the meanings to help you write definitions for your words.

   Greek: **photo** (light) **graph** (written) **tele** (distant) **gram** (recorded) **phone** (sound, voice)

   Latin: **cent** (hundred) **ject** (throw) **octo** (eight) **vac** (empty) **creat** (make)

   _____

   _____

   _____

2. Some words trace their origin to people's names. Use the clues to give the modern words.

   > For example, Sylvester Graham (1794–1851) helped develop a type of biscuit. We know it as a **graham cracker**.

   (a) Count Ferdinand von Zeppelin (1838–1917) developed this lighter-than-air ship.

   _____

   (b) This addictive substance, found in tobacco, is attributed to Jean Nicot (1530?–1600), a French diplomat.

   _____

   (c) Sir James Watt (1736–1819) gave us this word describing a unit of power, especially electrical.

   _____

   (d) The Roman goddess of agriculture, Ceres, gives us this word that generally describes a breakfast food.

   _____

   (e) The fourth Earl of Sandwich (1718–1792) developed this method of presenting food.

   _____

3. Select one of these words. Using a dictionary or other research material, trace its origin. Write your findings.

   flotsam   partial   world   travel   wilderness   Wednesday   August   epilepsy

   _____

   _____

 Trace the origin of your family name or trace the origin of an interesting word of your choice. Write your information down. Share it.

CHECK UP 1 ▸ *Vocabulary*

1. Add the **prefixes** and **suffixes** to the **root forms** to make new words. Make at least one new word for each root form.

   mid-   **im-**   **extra-**   **-ant**   **-ory**   **-ity**

   port:_____

   sense: _____

   way: _____

2. Give a **synonym** and an **antonym** for each word.

	evening	consistency	amateur	slow	vacant
synonym					
antonym					

3. Write three **homonym** pairs.

   _____   _____   _____

   _____   _____   _____

4. Use **similes** to complete these sentence fragments.

   (a) She jumped _____

   (b) We swam _____

   (c) I talked _____

5. Use **metaphors** to complete these sentence fragments.

   (a) The team _____

   (b) After the test, my mind _____

   (c) Our party _____

6. Select one of these things. Write a sentence about it using **personification**.
   box   star   wind   street   house

   _____

   _____

7. Match these **borrowed words** with their languages of origin. Use a dictionary if needed.
   French   Russian   Algonkian   Yiddish

   bagel: _____   steppe: _____

   toboggan: _____   chauffeur: _____

CHECK UP 2 ▸ *Colloquial English*

1. What is **colloquial English**?

   _____

   _____

2. Give two examples of **colloquial English**. Describe what each word/phrase means.

   _____ : _____

   _____ : _____

3. Rewrite these sentences using **colloquial English**.

   (a) The carton of books should be put on the shelf.

   _____

   (b) "We found a new type of fungus on our hike!" exclaimed Colton.

   _____

   (c) A very small pebble can cause countless ripples.

   _____

4. Write a short paragraph on a topic of your choice. Use as much **colloquial English** in your writing as you can.

   _____

   _____

   _____

   _____

   _____

   _____

   _____

   _____

   _____

   _____

   _____

   _____

   _____

UP 3 ▸ *Standard English*

1. What is **standard English**?

   _____

   _____

2. Give two examples of **standard English**. Describe what each word/phrase means.

   _____: _____

   _____: _____

3. Rewrite these sentences using **standard English**.

   (a) The guys kinda took their time gettin' here, you know?

   _____

   (b) Hey! Could you get my computer working again? Okay?

   _____

   (c) So, judging by how many times you're on the ground, how long you been skateboarding?

   _____

4. Write a short paragraph on a topic of your choice. Use mainly **standard English** in your writing.

   _____

   _____

   _____

   _____

   _____

   _____

   _____

   _____

   _____

   _____

   _____

   _____

CHECK UP 4 ▸ Formal and Informal Language

1. What is the difference between **formal** and **informal language**?

   _____

   _____

2. Write **formal** or **informal** beside each of the following situations to show what type of language should be used.

   (a) a doctor writing out a prescription: _____

   (b) writing out a recipe for a friend: _____

   (c) a telephone conversation with the school principal: _____

   (d) conversing in a Web site chat room: _____

   (e) giving directions to a tourist: _____

   (f) completing an essay for History class: _____

3. Rewrite these rules in **informal language**.

   (a) Look both ways before crossing the street.

   _____

   (b) Always stop when the traffic light is red.

   _____

   (c) Please don't walk on the grass.

   _____

   (d) You will be charged if you are caught travelling over the speed limit.

   _____

4. Rewrite these rules in **formal language**.

   (a) So, sign in at the office, you know, like when you're late, alright?

   _____

   (b) Like I've always said: Don't you ever—I mean ever—throw garbage on the street!

   _____

   (c) Yeah, I meant to tell you about getting docked an hour's pay if you're late for work.

   _____

   (d) So, a field goal's worth three points.

   _____

Unit 2

Spelling, Capitalization, Punctuation

FOCUS ON: Spelling

1. Circle the correctly spelled word in each group.

   - paterns   patterns   patturns   pattirns
   - memory   memoory   memmory   memorie
   - suspitious   suspichious   suspicious   suspicous
   - prefeerence   preferance   prefarence   preference
   - abreviation   abbreviation   abbreveation   abbreviasion

2. Proofread this paragraph for **spelling errors**. Circle any errors. Rewrite the paragraph with the correct spellings.

   > We decided to visit Ontario Place over the wekend. Cinespher was showina a filmnabout wolves. It seemed grate, but Micheline prferred to one on the Egyptians. Franco spent over an hour on the padel boats! What a nut! Me: I likd the maz—amazing!

   _____

   _____

   _____

   _____

   _____

3. Make these words **plural**.

   wolf: _____   octopus: _____

   baby: _____   sheep: _____

   child: _____   index: _____

   chief: _____   drape: _____

4. Write two sentences answering: What is your favourite movie? Why?

   Check your **spelling** after you have written the sentences.

   _____

   _____

   _____

   _____

   _____

FOCUS ON: Capitalization and Punctuation

1. Complete this statement with at least three ideas.

   Capital letters are used _____

   _____

2. Rewrite these sentences adding **capital letters** where needed.

   (a) i saw ms. johnson at the kilgaren concert hall on thursday.

   _____

   (b) We need to go down glover road to get to thames town by three.

   _____

3. Add the kind of **punctuation** indicated by the clues.

   (a) ends a sentence (3 kinds): _____ _____ _____

   (b) used to separate items in a list: _____ _____

   (c) used to indicate someone speaking: _____ _____

   (d) used in a contraction: _____

   (e) can be used to separate main clauses: _____

4. Add appropriate **punctuation** to these sentences.

   (a) Jeremy used pens markers and acetate to create a great visual effect

   (b) We know youre in there yelled the police chief

   (c) Ice cream is different it complements any meal

5. Rewrite these sentences adding **capital letters** and **punctuation** where needed.

   (a) mr barasek mrs wiley and burton flew from vancouver calgary and winnipeg on different flights

   _____

   _____

   (b) if only id bought tickets to the game sighed marie i would have seen valerie make that game winning shot

   _____

   _____

Spelling Rules

1. **Words ending in *e***: Drop the *e* when adding an ending or suffix beginning with a vowel. Keep the *e* if the suffix starts with a consonant.

    tame + ing = taming   same + ness = sameness

2. **Words ending in a consonant and *y***: Change the *y* to *i* before adding endings. Keep the *y* if the ending begins with *i*.

    beauty + ful = beautiful   fly + ing = flying

3. **Words ending in a vowel and *y***: Leave the *y* when adding endings.

    play + ing = playing

4. **One-syllable words**: If the word ends in a single vowel with a single consonant, double the consonant when you add an ending beginning with a vowel.

    stop + ing = stopping   slam + ed = slammed

5. **Multi-syllable words**: If the word ends with a single vowel and consonant, with the accent (stress) on the last syllable, double the consonant when you add an ending that begins with a vowel.

    begin + ing = beginning

6. **With *i* and *e***: Use *i* before *e* except after *c*, or when it sounds like *a* as in **sleigh**.

    receive   believe   weigh

These rules should help you in your spelling. However, here are some spelling and proofreading tips to think about as you spell words in your everyday writing.

- Read as much and as often as you can. This will show you the correct spellings of words used in context.

- Use a dictionary for spell checking.

- Use a computer spell checker, but remember that it will often give you many words to choose from. You need to have a good idea how to spell the word or you might choose one that doesn't fit your context.

- Read your work forwards and backwards, word for word, looking for words that don't look right.

- Use memory tricks to help you spell words: **This is so B-E-A-U-tiful!**

- Break larger words into their syllable parts. A dictionary will help you with this.

- Look for smaller words in larger ones: **TO - mor - ROW**

- Check the phonetic spellings of words to help you pronounce them correctly.

 Use the ideas on this page as a self-check whenever you spell words.

Use the rules and tips from p. 26 to help you with the activities on this page.

1. Add the endings to these words.

   wonder + ful = _____   trim + ing = _____

   flame + ing = _____   pot + ed = _____

   happy + ness = _____   make + er = _____

2. Break these words into **syllables**. Place an accent on the **stressed syllable**. Check your work in a dictionary.

   wonderful: _____   software: _____

   industry: _____   propeller: _____

   atomized: _____   trumpeter: _____

   catering: _____   graciously: _____

   immediately: _____   assignment: _____

3. Use a dictionary to give the **phonetic spellings** and **definitions** of these words.

   genesis: _____ ; _____

   infirmity: _____ ; _____

   longitudinal: _____ ; _____

   motocross: _____ ; _____

   pentahedron: _____ ; _____

   whisper: _____ ; _____

4. Write three sentences using at least three of the words listed in Activity #3.

   (a) _____

   _____

   _____

   (b) _____

   _____

   _____

   (c) _____

   _____

   _____

Use **proofreading tips** to help you in these activities.

1. **Proofread** these sentences for **spelling errors**. Highlight the misspelled words.

    (a) The computer crashed again laste nite after the power falure.

    (b) Whenevr I travell, I take an identifiasion card just inn cas.

    (c) "If he gets' the pass," Leo smild, "you takle him from the sidlines."

    > Spelling must be in the correct context, in the correct usage. If not, the word is technically misspelled.

2. Check this ad for **spelling errors**. Rewrite it in the box with corrected spelling.

    > **Available Now!**
    > **Everything Your Going**
    > **To Nead**
    > **For the Holidaze!**
    >
    > **Come to**
    > **Groupie Sportz**
    > **and get**
    > **Outfited for the**
    > **Nu Year!**

3. **Proofread** these movie listings. Rewrite them correcting any **spelling errors**.

    School Daze: A crazy romp thru the halls of Fortune High, were the kids 'r wild and the staf to milde!

    _____

    Filling in Time: Jennifer finds life too humerous as she taks up the dril to become the neihborhood dentist!

    _____

4. Make up your own movie listing, complete with film title. **Proofread** it, fixing any **spelling errors** you find.

    _____

    _____

    _____

    _____

    _____

 Check newspapers and magazines for any spelling errors. Highlight them.

Capitalization

Capital letters are required in a number of situations.

> When in doubt, check a dictionary to see if a word should be capitalized or not.

- **sentence beginnings**: The car drove past.
- **proper nouns**: Jeremy, Toronto
- **titles of movies, books, articles, and songs** (the major words): *Star Wars, Hamlet,* The End of the Day, Oh Canada
- **titles of persons**: Dr. Louise Kwon
- **in quotations**, at the beginning: "We had fun!" she said.

1. Make a list of five types of words (such as names) you feel need to be capitalized. Indicate why each needs **capital letters**.

   _____: _____

   _____: _____

   _____: _____

   _____: _____

   _____: _____

2. Write a word (or words) for each item. Use **capital letters** where necessary.

   a type of car: _____

   a book title: _____

   a TV show: _____

   a brand of clothing: _____

   a brand of cereal: _____

3. Proofread these sentences for use of **capital letters**. Circle where the capitals are needed. Rewrite the sentences with **capital letters**.

   (a) mr. canten, the custodian, found a copy of catcher in the rye in the planter.

   _____

   (b) star wars episode 1: the phantom menace was a religious experience for many moviegoers.

   _____

   _____

   (c) "we pride ourselves in being caring," said gena, "but canada could do much more for the third world."

   _____

   _____

Write a paragraph or two about a person in the news or an entertainment/media celebrity. Include at least:

- two titles of movies, books, songs, or articles;

> Remember not to overuse capital letters. They should be used just when necessary.

- five proper nouns;

- three titles of persons;

- two quotations, where characters are speaking.

Proofread your writing for **capitalization**, then for **spelling**. Give your writing to a friend to proofread as well.

_____

_____

_____

_____

_____

_____

_____

_____

_____

_____

_____

_____

_____

_____

_____

_____

_____

 Proofread an older piece of your writing for correct capitalization. Make any corrections needed.

 **Punctuation**

Sentences use **end punctuation** in two ways:

- to show where the sentence ends;
- to show the mood and vocal inflection of the sentence.

> The three types of **end punctuation** are:
> . period
> ? question mark
> ! exclamation mark

For example:

- a **period** indicates a calm, formal voice;

- a **question mark** indicates a questioning inflection, a rising of the voice;

- an **exclamation mark** indicates a forceful, enthusiastic, sometimes panicked voice.

1. Read these sentences out loud. Use the **end punctuation** to indicate the type of voice to use.

    (a) We met on vacation.

    (b) How long did you stay away?

    (c) It was way too long!

2. Add **end punctuation** to these sentences.

    (a) When is the game's start time____

    (b) I have a friend in Budapest____

    (c) Get out of here now____

    (d) So you have how many CD's____

    (e) I wish you'd stop talking____

    (f) Look over here____

3. Some sentences can end with either a **period** or an **exclamation mark**. Read these examples and indicate the **mood** of the speaker in each sentence.

    (a) I had a bad day. _____

    (b) I had a bad day! _____

4. Write a sentence that could end with either a **period** or an **exclamation mark**. Indicate the **mood** for each sentence.

    _____

    _____

    _____

    _____

▶▶ *Bring in the lyrics for a song which uses at least two types of end punctuation.*

Punctuation

Use **commas**:

> Don't overuse commas. These usage rules will help you decide where commas should go.

- **to separate three or more words in a list**: milk, bread, cakes, and cheese
- **to set off an introductory adverb clause**: When skateboarders find pavement, they turn it into a racetrack.
- **between adjectives of equal importance**: Desperate, frightened deer eyed the wolves.
- **to set off terms of direct address**: Dale, where were you today?
- **to separate parts of a place name, address, and date**: Toronto, Ontario, had incredible celebrations on December 31, 1999.

1. Insert **commas** into these sentences where needed.

   (a) The use of ropes hooks and lighted helmets are a must for spelunkers in the Carlsbad Caverns New Mexico.

   (b) Experienced knowledgeable cavers challenge the caves regularly.

   (c) As they descend into the cavern their lights are turned on.

   (d) Merle how long have you been a caver?

   (e) Since June 22 1993 I've been going into caves all around the world.

Commas are also used:

> An **appositive** is a noun or noun phrase giving additional information about the noun it is placed beside in a sentence.

- **to set off adjective clauses**: Gale, who had sailed the Atlantic, returned home.
- **to set off appositives**: Winnipeg, a Canadian city, is the capital of Manitoba.
- **before a conjunction joining two main clauses**: We enjoyed the film, and Louis critiqued the previews.
- **after a prepositional phrase**: Of all the days to have a storm, we had to get hit now!
- **after expressions that interrupt**: The long roads (e.g., Yonge Street) need special care.

2. Insert **commas** into these sentences where needed.

   (a) If you can do it we would appreciate a lift to Banff.

   (b) Nunavut the new territory is large in land mass and has a small population.

   (c) Rheam a fantastic place kicker won many a game (e.g. against Tech High).

   (d) I like ice cream but I can't stand spinach.

3. Write a sentence using at least one of the comma usages. Tell what usage rule it follows.

   _____

   _____

 Proofread newspaper articles to see if commas are used properly.

Punctuation

Apostrophes

Use an **apostrophe**:

- **to show possession**: the dog's bone; Kaitlyn's homework

- **to show where missing letters go in contractions**: didn't; wouldn't

- **to pluralize numbers**: 6's; 24's

- **to pluralize letters and words used as words**: too many no's

- **to pluralize abbreviations**: I.D.'s

> Apostrophes generally show possession.

> Apostrophes show missing letters.

1. Make **contractions** from these word pairs.

   will not: _____   she is: _____

   have not: _____   they are: _____

   I would: _____   I have: _____

2. Make **possessives** from these. For example, "the book of Doug" becomes Doug's book.

   the car of Jasmine: _____   the skates of Rene: _____

   the canoe of the team: _____   the gift of Serina: _____

   the score of the game: _____   the circle of the winner: _____

3. Add **apostrophes** where needed in these sentences.

   (a) You have too many nos and too few yess in this paragraph.

   (b) We vacationed in the winter of 99 at Jacks cottage.

   (c) Who has the IOUs?

   (d) Were all 6s and 9s today!

4. Write two sentences using at least two apostrophe usages. Tell which usages you used.

   (a) _____

   _____

   Usage: _____

   (b) _____

   _____

   Usage: _____

 Create some new contractions, such as *holiday not = holidan't.* ***Use them in sentences to show their meanings.***

Punctuation

A **colon** refers to what follows it. A **semicolon** is used to separate major sentence parts.

Look at these examples:

Colon

> A colon:
> • starts a list
> • links two main clauses where one explains or summarizes the other
> • precedes a formal quotation
> • separates hours and minutes, and chapter and verse references

- We need these things: a hammer, a saw, nails, wood, and a plan.

- Potatoes are a carbohydrate food: they are an excellent source of energy and vitamins.

- Hamlet said: "To be or not to be, that is the question."

- The time is 3:15 p.m. The verse is John 16: 3–5.

Semicolon

> A semicolon:
> • goes between two main clauses in a compound sentence not connected by a conjunction
> • separates items in a series when other punctuation is already used

- Harry enjoyed his work; it was his leisure time that needed attention.

- The team played well in Montreal, Quebec; Halifax, Nova Scotia; and Fredericton, New Brunswick.

1. Write three sentences using **colons** in each. Use the points above to help you.

   (a) _____

   _____

   (b) _____

   _____

   (c) _____

   _____

2. Write three sentences using **semicolons** in each. Use the points above to help you.

   (a) _____

   _____

   (b) _____

   _____

   (c) _____

   _____

3. Try this! Write one or two sentences that combine the use of **colons** and **semicolons**.

   _____

   _____

   _____

 Make a rule to help you know when to use a colon or a semicolon.

Punctuation

Quotation marks call attention to special parts of writing, usually speech.

Look at these examples:
- "I see we're all here," said Mickey.
- We started the meeting with "Oh Canada."

> Quotation marks:
> - enclose a direct quotation
> - enclose names of short works, such as short stories, essays, poems, and songs
> - enclose words or phrases used in a special sense, such as nicknames or slang. Do not overuse this.

1. Add **quotation marks** where needed to these sentences.

    (a) Derek always skiied well said Michelle. He just flew over the snow.

    (b) The name Snowman was given to him years ago.

    (c) His poem I Live for Snow was read by the whole team.

    (d) Why did he have to leave the ski team? asked Laura. Could it have anything to do with his move to the Amazon?

2. Quotations that appear within larger quotations are set off with **single quotation marks**.

    - "Derek 'The Snowman' was the best skier," said Laura.

    Add **quotation marks** where needed to these sentences.

    (a) Must we always read The Monkey's Paw? moaned Quigley.

    (b) I wish that Sneaky Simmons, aka Bert, would stop singing Imagine! yelled Connor.

3. Write a short conversation using **quotation marks**. Include at least one quotation within a quotation.

    _____

    _____

    _____

    _____

    _____

    _____

    _____

    _____

    _____

    _____

 Write a poem or song lyrics using quotation marks throughout.

Use this chart to see how **quotations** are **punctuated**.

Punctuating Quotations	Example
• comma ending the quotation and preceding the quotation mark	*"Jenny is being honoured for her outstanding academic achievement and her meals-for-seniors project," stated Mr. Khan.*
• comma before and after the tag when the speaker tag interrupts the quotation	*"All that work," I said, "is being rewarded."*
• question mark inside the quotation marks because it's part of the quote	*However, Jenny said, "What work?"*
• exclamation mark outside the quotation marks because the person quoting is exclaiming	*She actually said, "It was fun"!*
• as above, because the person quoting is questioning	*Did she really say, "It was fun"?*
• in a quoted passage of more than one paragraph, quotation marks opening all paragraphs but not ending any except the last	*"What makes people strive?," asked Jenny in her speech. She went on to answer, "Clear goals make people strive."* *"However, what makes a person continue to strive, to fight for life and honour? I believe, based on my visits to seniors in their homes, that strong relationships with family and friends are what really count."*

1. Add **quotations** and **punctuation** where needed to this conversation.

   I thought we had it all sighed Ramone the depth the players and the skill

   Well commented Jennie we didn't count on a better-trained team

   So what Ramone yelled We practised for weeks

   Yes, but we lost she replied and there's nothing we can do about it now.

2. Add **quotation marks** and **punctuation** where needed to these sentences.

   (a) Are you sure he said Disband the team

   (b) I thought he said Forget the game Gary replied

   (c) After hearing this I said Let's practise even harder

3. Write a short conversation using **quotation marks** and appropriate **punctuation**. Use the points in the chart to help you.

   _____

   _____

   _____

   _____

 ▶▶ *Rewrite one of your older pieces of writing as a conversation.*

Punctuation

Dashes, Parentheses, Ellipses

Dashes

- **show a change in thought**: He went this way—no, that way.

- **set off an interruption to the main idea**: The dance—only the best one—was over at midnight.

- **set off a summary of what came before or follows an inverted list**: Great food, music, dancing—all that Marci ever wanted.

Parentheses

- **enclose extra material or afterthoughts**: The game (to be played tomorrow) was important.

- **around letters or numbers in labelling**: They had to (1) fill the can, (2) carry it outside, and (3) dump it in the well.

Ellipses

- **show an interruption in dialogue**: "George Lucas was...well, he directed this," said the critic.

- **identify incomplete thoughts**: James sat and worried about his life, his work, his girlfriend...yet he didn't know what to do.

- **indicate words left out of a quotation**: "It was the best of times...it was the age of wisdom..."

Use **dashes**, **parentheses**, and **ellipses** to fix these sentences. Rewrite each sentence adding the appropriate punctuation.

1. Please remember: 1. take out the garbage, 2. put it at the curb, and 3. gather up the recycling.

   _____

2. I'm sure it's over there no wait, it's down this path.

   _____

3. The dog waited and waited and waited it was a long day.

   _____

4. We played well or so we thought but lost it in overtime.

   _____

5. That artist paints well, at least he paints.

   _____

6. Tent, stove, blankets, food they're some of the things you might use in an overnight hike.

   _____

 Look for examples of dashes, parentheses, and ellipses in everyday sources.

Capitalization, Punctuation *Usage 1*

1. Add **punctuation** and **capital letters** to the following paragraph:

See pp. 29–37 for capitalization and punctuation pointers.

we have so many choices today we can communicate in person on the telephone by e-mail and by snail mail I wonder what it was like when people couldn't talk to one another instantly if a family member moved some distance away the only way to keep in touch was by horse and buggy or to send a letter which would surely have taken quite some time to get there can you imagine how long it would take to share important news no wonder native people relied on smoke signals

_____

_____

_____

_____

_____

_____

_____

_____

2. Add **punctuation** and **capital letters** to the following paragraph:

the study of english is all about communication for centuries writers have been expressing their ideas in writing isnt it amazing how well their work has stood the test of time can you imagine writing something today which would last as long as to be or not to be from hamlet although we may have trouble understanding every single word that shakespeare wrote we certainly still enjoy seeing his work come alive onstage consider how many writers there are in the world today and how many books have been written since we were first able to record ideas and you have quite a number of people all communicating their thoughts and ideas mind boggling isnt it

_____

_____

_____

_____

_____

_____

_____

_____

Capitalization, Punctuation   *Usage 2*

Select one of these story ideas. Write a short piece that is at least three paragraphs long. Use proper **capitalization** and **punctuation**. Your story could be fiction or based on fact.

Story Ideas:

a favourite vacation	**a birthday**
the concert	**returning a gift**
in the news	**the lottery**
missing homework	**a dream**
end of the year	**not enough cash**

CHECK UP 1 Spelling

1. A **spelling rule** is: *i before e*, **except after c.** Write three more spelling rules.

   (a) _____

   (b) _____

   (c) _____

2. A **spelling tip** is: **Read your work backwards to check for misspelled words.** Write two more spelling tips. One of them could be your own idea.

   (a) _____

   (b) _____

3. Circle the **correctly spelled word** in each group.
   - symputhetic   simpathetic   sympathetic   sympathitic
   - endeavoured   endevoured   endavored   endeavourd
   - enamul   enaemel   enamml   enamel
   - mysterry   mystery   mistery   mysterie
   - momenterily   momentarly   momentarily   momentrily

4. (a) **Pluralize** these words.

   child: _____   chef: _____   class: _____

   wolf: _____   man: _____   guitar: _____

   (b) Add the **endings** to these words.

   beauty + ful = _____   announce + ment = _____

   crazy + ness = _____   stop + ing = _____

5. Circle the **spelling errors** in these sentences. Rewrite the sentences with the words correctly spelled.

   (a) The onley way I was going to desend into the cave was by a stif rop!

   _____

   (b) Thay lowrd me down into the drkness, and I was a bit scarried!

   _____

   (c) Insid the cave was beutiful, yet I stil felt asif sumthing was down their with me!

   _____

CHECK UP 2 ▸ *Capitalization*

1. Describe three situations when **capital letters** are used.

   (a) _____

   (b) _____

   (c) _____

2. Write five examples of words, names, or titles that use **capital letters**. Explain why each needs a capital.

   (a) _____ : _____

   (b) _____ : _____

   (c) _____ : _____

   (d) _____ : _____

   (e) _____ : _____

3. Proofread this paragraph for use of **capital letters**. Circle the letters that need to be capitalized. Rewrite the paragraph using capitals where you indicated.

   it was a glorious night when we went to campbell's theatre to see demented dogs in concert. our friends, tina and jermaine, had arrived at 8:00. they took carlin street; we went along mason avenue and were fifteen minutes late—what geeks! anyway, the concert went well, but the dogs didn't do justice to their hit, canine love. it was a bit droll. oh well, at least our burgers at pattie's burgers dining palace were a definite a–1 hit!

   _____

   _____

   _____

   _____

   _____

   _____

   _____

   _____

   _____

   _____

   _____

1. Give the three types of **end punctuation** and the types of sentences they end.

   (a) _____: _____

   (b) _____: _____

   (c) _____: _____

2. Use proper **end punctuation** to finish these sentences.

   (a) We went to the party___

   (b) Where is everybody___

   (c) I can't find the light switch___

   (d) Surprise___

   (e) If I had known, I'd have baked a cake___

   (f) So, the presents you got are where___

   (g) Why doesn't anyone care that I hate cologne___

   (h) Look, calm down___

   (i) Okay, it's only a party___

   (j) You're right, and a great one at that___

3. Write a sentence that could be completed with two different **end punctuation** marks. Indicate the sentence's mood for each.

   _____

   _____

   _____

   _____

4. Write an advertisement or a poem that uses all three types of **end punctuation**. Use your **end punctuation** effectively.

   _____

   _____

   _____

   _____

   _____

Internal Punctuation

1. Name each of these **punctuation** marks.

   " "   ʻ   ,   :

   _____   _____   _____   _____

        ;   —   ...   ( )

   _____   _____   _____   _____

2. Add **punctuation** where needed to these sentences. Rewrite each sentence with the correct punctuation.

   (a) Where are we? asked Jules.

   _____

   (b) It is that time and we all know it has come.

   _____

   (c) I wont gather flowers stems or pebbles actually if Im paid I will.

   _____

   (d) He had a frightening experience it left him speechless.

   _____

   (e) What we need is this a better song some better players a better manager yes I think thats it!

   _____

   (f) The ship the *Mary Claire* sailed off with crew passengers and cargo that fateful day.

   _____

3. Write sentences or a short paragraph that uses all of the **punctuation** marks in Activity #1. Use each mark at least once.

   _____

   _____

   _____

   _____

   _____

   _____

   _____

   _____

   _____

   _____

Unit 3

Grammar and Usage

FOCUS ON: Grammar

1. Match these **pronouns** with the nouns.

   they   her   he   it

   Ricardo: _____   Sheila's: _____

   girls: _____   CN Tower: _____

2. In these sentences, circle the **verbs**.

   (a) The horse galloped across the plain.

   (b) We flew from Montreal to Regina.

   (c) What is the time?

   (d) I found my homework!

   (e) We are going to win this time!

3. In these sentences, circle any **adjectives** and underline any **adverbs**.

   (a) The long hot day dragged on slowly.

   (b) There were brown, rusty pieces of metal everywhere.

   (c) At three o'clock, we will leave for the coast.

4. In these sentences, draw a line between the **subject** and the **predicate**.

   (a) The lonely aardvark ambled onto the highway.

   (b) A smaller version of the toy was sold at the auction.

   (c) We come in peace.

   (d) At last the crew landed on the desolate planet.

   (e) Far too many shoppers returned their presents after the holiday season.

5. Combine each group of shorter sentences into one sentence. Write the new sentence on the line.

   (a) I saw the hit. I caught the ball.

   _____

   (b) Steve slid into homeplate. We had a tie game!

   _____

   (c) The ball was hit. I jumped up. It landed in my glove.

   _____

   (d) Jason threw three strikes. It was the final out. We won.

   _____

46

Parts of Speech

A **noun** is a word that names a person, place, or thing.

stove	Michelle	Derek	hockey	friendship
faith	Rolling Stones	strawberry		

> A noun can be
> • common (names a person, place, or thing)
> • proper (the name of a person, place, or thing)

1. Write a proper noun for each common noun.

   street: _____   uncle: _____

   city: _____   singer: _____

   country: _____   team: _____

   girl: _____   car: _____

   aunt: _____   cereal: _____

2. Nouns can be singular (one of something) or plural (more than one of something).

   bird/birds   calf/calves

   • Most noun plurals add **s**. If a noun ends in **ch, s, sh,** or **z**, add **es**.

   • If a noun ends in **y**, change **y** to **i** and then add **es**.

   • If a noun ends in **f** or **fe**, change the **f** or **fe** to **v** and add **es** (except **chief**).

   Make these nouns plural.

   life: _____   dress: _____

   kid: _____   dish: _____

   cosmonaut: _____   buzz: _____

   wolf: _____   lady: _____

3. A **compound noun** has two or more smaller words in it. It is written as one word, joined with a hyphen, or given as separate words.

   rainbow   daughter-in-law   Backstreet Boys

   Write a sentence using at least two types of compound nouns.

   _____

   _____

4. **Possessive nouns** show ownership.

   > A possessive noun uses an apostrophe and **s**.

   Jim's store   the lady's gloves

   Rewrite these using possessive nouns.

   the book of Darla: _____   the CD of Calley: _____

   the motorbike of Kaitlyn: _____   the lunch of the student: _____

▶▶ *Write a paragraph about a topic of interest to you and underline all of the nouns you used.*

A **pronoun** is a word that takes the place of a noun.

Pronouns can also take the place of other pronouns or groups of words.

Germaine saw the coat and **she** bought **it**. (**she** replaces Germaine; **it** replaces coat)

1. Rewrite these sentences, replacing the boldfaced nouns with **pronouns**.

    (a) Denise left the box, but **Denise** didn't need the **box** until tomorrow.

    _____

    (b) Laura had a book about **Laura's** family.

    _____

    (c) The players worked hard and played well, but the **players** lost the game as the **game** entered the final minutes.

    _____

    _____

2. **Possessive pronouns** show ownership.

    her book   **his radio**   **their party**   **its stall**

    Write a sentence using at least one possessive pronoun.

    _____

    _____

3. Some pronouns use **self**: **myself, herself, himself, itself**; or plural: **themselves, ourselves**.

    Write a sentence using at least one **self** pronoun.

    _____

    _____

4. Other pronouns include: **who, whom, whomever, whose, what, this, that, these, those, another, anyone, each, either, neither, nothing, no one, somebody, both, few, all, any, most, none.**
    Write two sentences using at least four of these pronouns.

    _____

    _____

    _____

    _____

 Write a short piece using all of the pronouns in Activity #4. Does it make sense?

Parts of Speech   *Noun, Pronoun Agreement*

Nouns and pronouns must **agree** or refer correctly to each other. For example,

| A **pronoun** refers to a word or group of words. This is the pronoun's antecedent. |

John saw the TV. **They** turned it on. (**They** is plural; it does not refer correctly to John.)

John saw the TV. **He** turned it on. (**He** is singular; it refers correctly to John.)

1. For each of these sentences, indicate the **noun** that each pronoun refers to. Circle the **pronouns**. Draw lines from each **pronoun** to its **antecedent**.

    (a) Maria found her way to the mall because it was on her route.

    (b) The students rushed into their seats, grabbed their headphones, and began listening to the newest CD as it played for them.

    (c) Marco said he found them at the park and the children were happy they weren't lost anymore.

2. (a) Write at least one **pronoun** for each **antecedent**.

    Gina: _____

    shopping mall: _____

    NASA: _____

    computer program: _____

    NHL: _____

    parents: _____

    hiking equipment: _____

    movies: _____

    (b) Select some of the noun/pronoun pairs from above. Use them in three sentences. You could put your sentences together in a short paragraph.

    _____

    _____

    _____

    _____

    _____

 Can an entire piece of writing use only pronouns? Try it! See how far you can get without referring to any nouns.

Parts of Speech

Verbs

A **verb** is a word that shows action or being.

crash—shows action: The waves **crash** on the shore.

feel—shows a state of being: I **feel** better now.

> Some verbs are helpers:
> I   may   go.
> (helper) (main verb)

1. (a) Some action verbs are: **hit, run, walk, eat, jump, slam, dance**. Write down at least five more. _____

   (b) Some being verbs are: **be, am, is, are, was, were, become, seem**. Write down at least three more. _____

   (HINT: Check your words in a dictionary to see if you are correct.)

2. Verbs need to agree with their subjects. They agree in **number** (singular or plural) and in **person**.

	Singular	**Plural**
First person	I **shiver**	we **shiver**
Second person	you **shiver**	you **shiver**
Third person	he/she/it [for any singular noun] **shivers**	they [or any plural noun] **shiver**

   Underline the **correct verb** in parentheses for each sentence.
   (a) John (wait, waits) for his friends on the corner.
   (b) They (gives, give) him a lift to work.
   (c) At work, everyone (make, makes) cupholders for cars.
   (d) I (work, works) there with John.

3. Write sentences using these verbs. Check that your **verbs** agree with their **subjects** in number and person. Use **helper verbs** if necessary.

   is: _____

   _____

   charge: _____

   _____

   date: _____

   _____

   remain: _____

   _____

   journey: _____

   _____

▶▶ *Choose a new article and list which kinds of verbs are used most often.*

Parts of Speech

Active/Passive Voice

Action verbs have two voices:

- active voice: Dirt bikers **ride** their bikes over rough ground.
- passive voice: Bikes **are ridden** by dirt bikers over rough ground.

> **Active voice**: subject performs the action.
>
> **Passive voice**: subject receives the action using a form of the verb **be**.

1. Identify each sentence's verb as being in the **active voice** or the **passive voice**.

    (a) Nikko jumped into the water. _____

    (b) The pool was cleaned by Jeanette. _____

    (c) Our vacation was ruined by bad weather. _____

    (d) Snow pelted the car's windshield. _____

    (e) The motorists were stranded by the storm. _____

2. Rewrite these sentences in the **active voice**.

    (a) The ground was shaken by the earthquake.

    _____

    (b) Many buildings were destroyed in just a few seconds.

    _____

    (c) Residents were taken to all the local hospitals by every available ambulance.

    _____

3. Rewrite these sentences in the **passive voice**.

    (a) Doctors worked night and day on the victims.

    _____

    (b) Rescuers saved hundreds of people trapped in the rubble.

    _____

    (c) The earthquake devastated the area.

    _____

4. Write a sentence on any topic using the **active voice**. Rewrite it using the **passive voice**.

    (a) _____

    (b) _____

 Select a piece of writing you did a while ago. Experiment with the verb voice in it by alternating the active and passive voice throughout. Determine which works best for you.

 # Parts of Speech

Verb tense is used to show the time of its action.
The three main tenses are:

- **present**: happens   am
- **past:**   happened   was
- **future:**   will happen   will be

> Past tense adds **-ed** in most cases.
> Future tense uses **will** or **shall** as a helper verb.

1. Give the **past** and **future** tense of each of these **present** verbs.

   stop: _____ , _____

   leap: _____ , _____

   walk: _____ , _____

   smile: _____ , _____

   yell: _____ , _____

   sprint: _____ , _____

   say: _____ , _____

   sit: _____ , _____

   find: _____ , _____

   reply: _____ , _____

2. Select one of the verbs in Activity #1, or a new verb of your choice. Write three sentences for the verb: **present tense**, **past tense**, **future tense**.

   (a) _____

   _____

   (b) _____

   _____

   (c) _____

   _____

3. Here are two more **verb tenses**:
   - **present perfect tense**: has recently happened
   - **past perfect tense**: had happened

   Rewrite these sentences using the **present perfect tense**, then the **past perfect tense**.

   > Perfect tenses show action or a condition that
   > - occurred in the past and continued to the present: use **have** or **has**
   > - ended before another past action began: use **had**

   (a) Sean jumps into the water.

   _____

   (b) The player scores a goal.

   _____

 Rewrite a song lyric or an ad, changing the verb tense.

Parts of Speech

An **adjective** is a word that describes, or modifies, a noun, pronoun, or another adjective.

great game   **slow-moving** car

These are also adjectives: **the**, **a**, **an**; **this**, **that**, **these**, **those**; proper adjectives formed from proper nouns: **Asian** countries, **Elizabethan** era; comparative (**-er**) and superlative adjectives (**-est**): **fast**, **faster**, **fastest**.

> Adjectives are meant to create better mental pictures. They tell
> • how many
> • which one
> • what kind

> Some comparative and superlative adjectives use
> • more, most: **more arid**, **most arid**
> • less, least: **less arid**, **least arid**
> Some are irregular: **good**, **better**, **best**.

1. Give at least two **adjectives** describing each word, to help create better mental pictures.

    meal: _____

    game: _____

    vacation: _____

    show: _____

    singer: _____

2. Rewrite these sentences adding **adjectives** to improve the descriptions.

    (a) The group played their hit song to the crowd.

    _____

    (b) A watermelon was seen flying above their faces.

    _____

    (c) People started throwing chairs at the stage.

    _____

    (d) The concert ended in turmoil as the crowd raced for the exits.

    _____

    (e) The band, oblivious to this, played as if nothing had happened.

    _____

3. Write a short paragraph on a subject of your choice. Use **adjectives** to help make your descriptions more vivid.

    _____

    _____

    _____

    _____

 Describe, with inventive adjectives, how your day usually begins.

Parts of Speech

An **adverb** is a word that describes, or modifies, a verb, and adjective, or another adverb.

charged **quickly** (how)   arrived **late** (when)

flew **overhead** (where)   was **very** sick (to what extent)

> Adverbs usually answer the questions
> • how?
> • when?
> • where?
> • to what extent?
> Many adverbs are formed by adding **-ly** to an adjective:
> • quick: **quickly**

1. Write at least two **adverbs** for each of these verbs. Remember: how? when? where? to what extent?

   disagree: _____

   walked: _____

   speak: _____

   tumble: _____

   follow: _____

2. Read these sentences. Circle any **adverbs**.

   > Some adverbs come in phrases:
   > • walked <u>over there</u>
   > • talked <u>for an hour</u>

   (a) The lion meandered slowly into the pride.

   (b) She was very cold after swimming across Lake Ontario.

   (c) Watchful eyes really scared Tim, especially if they opened wide quickly.

3. **Adverbs** have **comparative** (**-er**) and **superlative** (**-est**) forms.

   late   later   latest   seldom   more seldom   most seldom
   good/well   better   best

   Write sentences using the **comparative** and **superlative** forms of these adverbs.

   (a) early: _____

   _____

   (b) warmly: _____

   _____

   (c) well: _____

   _____

4. Write a short descriptive paragraph. Use **adverbs** to help make your descriptions more vivid.

   _____

   _____

   _____

   _____

   _____

▶▶ *How do you describe yourself? Use interesting adverbs to give a character sketch of who you are.*

Parts of Speech

Conjunctions

A **conjunction** is a word that connects two or more words or group of words together.

The ball was caught **and** thrown to home plate.

People lined up **because** the tickets were about to be sold.

Some **conjunctions** are: and, but, or, nor, for, yet, so, after, although, if, since, so, that, unless, and while.

1. Using **conjunctions** from the side panel, join these sentences together. Rewrite the new sentences on the lines.

   (a) The ball was snapped. The quarterback passed it.

   _____

   (b) We saw the restaurant. It was too crowded.

   _____

   (c) The traffic was heavy. We enjoyed the weekend away.

   _____

2. Using **conjunctions** from the side panel and your own words, complete these sentences.

   (a) The drivers slammed on their brakes _____

   _____

   (b) The plane landed_____

   _____

   (c) Everyone saw the fireworks _____

   _____

   (d) The band members stood on stage _____

   _____

3. **Correlative conjunctions** work in pairs:

   Either this is not a joke, **or** I am getting too old for humour.

   Some conjunction pairs are: **either...or**; **neither...nor**; **both...and**; **just as...so (too)**; **not only...but (also)**; **whether...or**.

   Use **conjunction pairs** in three sentences.

   (a) _____

   _____

   (b) _____

   _____

   (c) _____

   _____

 Rewrite some of your sentences in Activities #2 and #3 with different conjunctions. How is the meaning of each sentence changed?

Parts of Speech

Prepositions

A **preposition** is a word that relates a noun or pronoun to another word in the sentence.

We ran toward the lake. (**toward** relates **the lake** to **ran**)

> Some **prepositions** are: against, about, above, along, among, between, but, except, like, over, since, through, to, toward, without, with, at, from, of, up, by means of, and according to.

1. Complete these sentences with **prepositions** from the side panel.

    (a) They drove _____ the shoreline.

    (b) Many skiers skied _____ the trees.

    (c) Hopeful concert goers bought tickets _____ the headliner act had cancelled.

    (d) Lava flowed _____ the desperate village.

    (e) She arrived home _____ her ability to never give up.

2. **Prepositions** also start phrases:

    of the dog: The snarl **of the dog** scared the cat.

    from a far distance: Jacob saw **from a far distance**.

    Use **prepositional phrases** to complete these sentences.

    (a) The crowd _____ swarmed onto the field.

    (b) We were covered with mud _____ .

    (c) Many groups _____ climbed the hill _____ .

3. Write a short paragraph on one of these topics. Use **prepositions** to relate words to one another.

    the concert   **a championship game**   **shopping at the mall**   **returning a gift**

    winning a lottery   **going on a first date**   **stuffing more things in the locker**

    _____

    _____

    _____

    _____

    _____

    _____

    _____

    _____

    _____

    _____

▶▶ ***Read through a newspaper or magazine article, counting how many times prepositions are used.***

Parts of Speech

An **interjection** is a word used to express a strong feeling or to get attention.

It is a part of everyday speech. In writing, interjections are used informally.

> Some **interjections** are: hey, oh, ha, ya, wow, all right, okay, oops, uh-oh, eh, and shhh.

Hey! I thought you were lost.

Oops! I dropped the cake.

Okay?

1. Add **interjections** to these sentences.

> Interjections usually appear at the beginning of a sentence, or on their own.

   (a) _____ My exam is finished!

   (b) _____ We have a winner!

   (c) _____ I'll bet you never had escargot.

   (d) _____ What are you doing?

   (e) _____ We have to be quiet.

   (f) _____ Here comes trouble!

   (g) _____ You win!

   (h) _____, so I didn't get the right thing.

   (i) _____, what if we fake an illness?

   (j) _____, I know: we're supposed to find a way out of this maze.

2. Write a short dialogue between two characters, using **interjections** when appropriate.

   _____

   _____

   _____

   _____

   _____

   _____

   _____

   _____

   _____

   _____

 Write a short piece or dialogue that uses interjections on their own, without any other words. Can it be done?

Sentences

There are four kinds of **sentences**, each with a different purpose.

- **declarative:** makes a statement and ends with a period, e.g., The ship sailed into the harbour.

- **interrogative**: asks a question and ends with a question mark, e.g., When did the ship arrive?

- **imperative:** makes a request or gives a command. The subject **you** is understood but not given. This sentence usually ends with a period: (You) Greet the ship's captain.

- **exclamatory:** expresses strong feeling and ends with an exclamation mark, e.g., I always have to greet the captain! Why me! Greet the captain now!

> Declarative, interrogative, and imperative sentences can be exclamatory if they express strong emotions and end with exclamation marks.

Write two of **each kind of sentence**. Indicate which kind each sentence is. You may want to write your sentences as a brief story.

_____

_____

_____

_____

_____

_____

_____

_____

_____

_____

_____

_____

_____

_____

 Write a short dialogue or conversation using two or more characters, using only exclamatory sentences.

Sentences

Simple

A simple sentence has a **subject** and a *predicate*.

A simple sentence has its subject and predicate in one main clause.

We *travelled to the Rockies.* The taxi driver *knew his way to the theatre.*

1. Complete these subjects with predicates to make simple sentences.

   (a) The soccer team _____

   (b) Everyone _____

   (c) A tall vase _____

   (d) Many buffalo _____

   (e) Every computer _____

2. Add **subjects** to these **predicates** to make **simple sentences**.

   (a) _____ found buried treasure on Oak Island.

   (b) _____ yelled "Surprise!"

   (c) _____ raced past the other runners.

   (d) _____ was very happy with the gift.

   (e) _____ watched the hornets' nest fall down.

Simple sentences can be
• declarative
• interrogative
• imperative, or
• exclamatory.

3. Write **simple sentences** on these topics.

   (a) an assembly: _____

   _____

   (b) lockers: _____

   _____

   (c) cafeteria food: _____

   _____

   (d) friends: _____

   _____

   (e) a dream: _____

   _____

   (f) changing classes: _____

   _____

   (g) the test: _____

   _____

   (h) the supply teacher: _____

   _____

 ▶▶ *Write a simple poem using only simple sentences.*

Sentences

Compound

A **compound sentence** is made from two simple sentences joined by a conjunction or a semicolon.

Reese poured the milk. She sat down to breakfast.

Reese poured the milk **and** sat down to breakfast.

> Each simple sentence in a compound sentence is an independent main clause. A compound sentence is made up of two independent main clauses.

1. Make a **compound sentence** from each pair of simple sentences

> A list of conjunctions can be found on p. 55.

   (a) The car swerved. It hit an embankment.

   _____

   _____

   (b) People lined the streets. The parade passed by.

   _____

   _____

   (c) We're having fun. The party will last until dawn.

   _____

   _____

   (d) She tried her best. She almost passed the test.

   _____

   _____

2. Write the **simple sentences** that make up each compound sentence.

   (a) The train left the station, yet we felt sad leaving.

   _____

   _____

   (b) A storm broke out, although good weather had been forecast.

   _____

   _____

   (c) Janine scored a goal, and the game went into overtime.

   _____

   _____

3. Write two **compound sentences**. Underline the simple sentences that make up your compound sentences.

   (a) _____

   (b) _____

Sentences

Complex

> A complex sentence is made up of one main clause and one or more subordinate clauses.

A complex sentence has one main simple sentence.
It has at least one other simple sentence that is **dependent** (or relies) on the main sentence.

As he stopped at the corner, a car whooshed by.
(dependent simple sentence) (main simple sentence)
    subordinate clause   main clause

> Place the dependent clause at the beginning before the main clause.

1. Create **complex sentences** by adding a main simple sentence to these dependent simple sentences.

    (a) Although the vehicles had been sold, _____

    _____

    (b) As the sun slowly set in the west, _____

    _____

    (c) Whenever our team scored a touchdown, _____

    _____

    (d) When the strange-looking animal jumped out from the behind the tree, _____

    _____

    (e) By the light of a dimly lit desk lamp, _____

    _____

    (f) Since the beginning of the movie was so lame, _____

    _____

    (g) When spring comes and new flowers grow, _____

    _____

    (h) As the ship sailed past the crowd, _____

    _____

2. Write four **complex sentences**. Remember where to place the **dependent clause**.

    (a) _____

    _____

    (b) _____

    _____

    (c) _____

    _____

    (d) _____

    _____

 Underline the main simple sentence in each of your four complex sentences above.

Sentences

The **subject** of a sentence is **who** or **what** the sentence is about. It consists of at least one noun or pronoun and any modifiers.

I enjoyed the show. **The audience** enjoyed the show. **Everyone in the theatre** enjoyed the show.

> The simple subject is usually one word.
> It is the main element or idea of the subject.
> **I, audience,** and **Everyone** are simple subjects.

1. Underline the **subjects** in these sentences. Circle the **simple subject** in each sentence.

   (a) A large, brown dog chased a cat down the street.

   (b) We jumped at the chance to go.

   (c) Every minute brings us closer to reality.

   (d) The white billowing sails of the three-masted clipper ship unfurled in the ocean breeze.

   (e) A fine mist of rain wet the spectators seated in the stands.

2. **Compound subjects** are linked together. For example,

   The heavy **boxes** and the delicate **vases** crashed to the floor.

   Boxes and **vases** make up a compound simple subject. What is the complete compound subject in the sentence?

   _____

   Underline the **complete compound subject** in this sentence. Circle the **compound simple subject** words.

   A flock of birds and a herd of antelope moved in the same direction.

3. Write a short paragraph with sentences that use **compound subjects**. Not all of your sentences need to have compound subjects.

   _____

   _____

   _____

   _____

   _____

   _____

   _____

   _____

   _____

 Experiment with making your subjects interesting and in different styles.

Sentences

The **predicate** is the verb of the sentence. It also includes modifiers and other parts of the sentence that are not part of the subject.

A simple predicate is the single verb (or the main and helping verbs). **Zoomed** and **were laughing** are simple predicates.

The low-flying plane **zoomed overhead**. We **were laughing at the comedian**.

1. Underline the **predicates** in these sentences. Circle the **simple predicate** in each sentence.

   (a) Balloons burst over the heads of the partiers.

   (b) Every motorist on the highway slowed down at the crash site.

   (c) The leader halted the group at the cave's entrance.

   (d) A crazy flip of the coin had cost us the game.

   (e) Mountains of water crashed through the crack in the dam.

2. **Compound predicates** are linked together. For example,

   Airplanes **soar** over the field and **dive** toward the crowd.

   Soar and **dive** are the verbs linked together. What is the full compound predicate in the sentence?

   _____

   Underline the **compound predicate** in the following sentence. Circle the **verbs** that are linked together.

   A whale jumped through the waves, then sounded to the water's depths.

3. Write a short paragraph that uses **compound predicates** where possible.

   _____

   _____

   _____

   _____

   _____

   _____

   _____

   _____

   _____

   _____

 How many verbs can you link together in a sentence? Try it! Make sure that your sentence makes sense and isn't cumbersome.

Sentences

Sentences can have two types of object.

> An object is a noun or pronoun that receives action from the subject after an action verb.

- **direct object:** noun or pronoun receives the action directly from the subject; answers **whom** or **what**: Drew sent a **postcard**. (direct object answering **what**)

- **indirect object:** noun or pronoun receives the action indirectly; answers **to what, for what, to whom**, or **for whom**: Drew send his **boss** a postcard. OR Drew sent a postcard to his **boss**. (Indirect object answering **to what**)

1. Underline the **direct objects** in these sentences.

   (a) The ball cracked the glass.

   (b) Birds ate the seeds from the lawn.

   (c) The diver climbed the ladder.

   (d) We ate the sandwiches with gusto!

   (e) A biker raced past Jeremy.

2. Underline the **indirect objects** in these sentences.

   (a) Hailey delivered boxes to Raymond.

   (b) The store clerk packaged the gift for the customer.

   (c) Drake fed seeds to the birds.

   (d) Jennifer jumped hurdles for the team.

   (e) He bought his wife flowers.

3. Write a short paragraph with sentences that use **direct** and **indirect objects**. Underline the **objects** in the sentences.

   _____

   _____

   _____

   _____

   _____

   _____

   _____

   _____

   _____

   _____

 Read through articles in newspapers, magazines, and other print materials, highlighting direct and indirect objects.

Sentences

A **subject complement** follows a linking verb. It describes the subject.

Huge waves are dangerous.
   (subject)   (subject complement)

Jennifer has a car.
(subject)   (subject complement)

> **Subject complements** are:
> • nouns,
> • pronouns, or
> • adjectives.

1. Underline the **subject complement** in each sentence.

    (a) The team became confident.

    (b) Our exam is difficult.

    (c) The weather seems worse.

    (d) The wayward traveller felt exhausted.

    (e) Avalanches are frequent on this side of the mountain.

2. Add a **subject complement** to complete each sentence fragment.

    (a) Kwan appears _____

    (b) The driver was _____

    (c) We are _____

    (d) The pizza seems _____

    (e) Shopping malls are _____

3. Underline the **subject complements** in this conversation. Add at least two more sentences to the conversation, using subject complements.

    "I am beat!" sighed Rohan.

    "How did it go today?" asked Philip.

    "Our band felt ready, but we just blew the audition," Rohan replied.

    "My audition was a failure," said Philip. "We couldn't do anything right."

    "We were too scared to play! What do you think of that?"

    _____

    _____

    _____

    _____

    _____

Write a poem about how you feel. Use subject complements. For example,
I feel outrageous!, I feel ridiculous!

A **main clause** makes sense as a sentence on its own.

> All sentences are made up of clauses.

The store stocked new merchandise.   (main clause)

A **subordinate clause** does not make sense as a sentence on its own. It must be linked to a main clause.

which will be sold during its sidewalk sale (subordinate clause)

> Main and subordinate clauses both have subjects and predicates.

Clauses together: The store stocked new merchandise which will be sold during its sidewalk sale.

1. Write **main** or **subordinate** after each clause to indicate its type.

    > Three types of subordinate clauses are:
    > • noun clause,
    > • adjective clause,
    > • adverb clause.

    (a) While playing rugby on the field _____

    (b) Whose name is Reilly _____

    (c) A car swerved on the ice. _____

    (d) He slammed into the boards. _____

2. Add a **main clause** to each **subordinate clause** to make a complete sentence.

    (a) While fishing off the bridge, _____

    (b) _____
         who want to learn how to play the guitar.

    (c) When the movie opened last week, _____

3. Add a **subordinate clause** to each **main clause** to make a complete sentence.

    > **Subordinate clauses** can start with these words:
    > that, which, whomever, how, where, what, who, whose, when, after, as soon as, so that, although, unless, as if, as though.

    (a) We found the trail _____
         _____

    (b) _____
         the dog barked and growled at the door.

    (c) A slow-moving train whistled in the distance _____

4. Write three sentences that use **main** and **subordinate clauses** in each sentence.

    (a) _____
         _____

    (b) _____
         _____

    (c) _____
         _____

▶ ▶ *Write out a song lyric or short magazine piece and identify the subordinate clauses.*

Sentences

A **prepositional phrase** begins with a preposition. It includes a noun or pronoun as the object.

The runner **with the best conditioning** will win the race.

> **Prepositions** include: against, above, along, among, between, but, like, over, of, since, from, by, into, according to, because of, to.

1. Underline the **prepositional phrases** in these sentences.

   (a) The oil tanker ran aground among the bay's rocks.

   (b) Mountain climbers with great skill have scaled these cliffs since I was a young girl.

   (c) The passage of time keeps all of us alert because of our desire to stay young.

   (d) A slight breeze moved between the walls, then shifted up over the boy standing by the side of the road.

   (e) Many shark pups were set free into the current along with other sea life.

> The object of the preposition is the noun or pronoun that the preposition relates to in the sentence. In "The runner with the best conditioning will win the race," **with** relates **conditioning** to **runner**.

2. Circle the **object** of the preposition in each phrase. Draw a line to the word it relates to.

   (a) The team from Tobermory won the championship.

   (b) A single ripple started with a pebble.

   (c) The dog stood between the two friends.

3. Rewrite these sentences adding **prepositional phrases** to make them more interesting and descriptive.

   (a) We drove. _____

   _____

   (b) The car stalled.

   _____

   _____

   (c) A mechanic opened the door.

   _____

   _____

   (d) She checked the water hoses.

   _____

   _____

   (e) The bill drained our resources.

   _____

   _____

 Practise placement of prepositional phrases in three of your own sentences. Make sure you write them close to the words they describe.

Sentences
Phrases: Adjective and Adverb

Adjective phrases describe, or modify, nouns or pronouns.
The pilot **from Moosonee** flew into the North Country.
(**from Moosonee** describes the noun "pilot"; answers "who?")

Adverb phrases describe, or modify, verbs or other adverbs.
The pilot from Moosonee flew **into the North Country**.
(**into the North Country** describes the verb "flew"; answers "where?")

> Adjective and adverb phrases are prepositional phrases.

1. Underline **adjective** and **adverb phrases** in these sentences. Write down which words they describe.

   (a) The gust of wind whipped past the explorers at three o'clock.

   _____

   (b) You, with the rope, will have to rescue the party at the summit.

   _____

   (c) A crazy hop of the puck sent the game into overtime.

   _____

2. Rewrite these sentences, adding **adjective** and **adverb phrases** to make them more vivid.

   (a) The goat ran.

   _____

   (b) Our bus arrived.

   _____

   (c) The class ended.

   _____

   (d) A torrential rain fell.

   _____

   (e) A delighted emcee introduced the acts.

   _____

3. Write a short descriptive paragraph on one of these topics. Use **adjective** and **adverb phrases** in your descriptions.

   **making a pizza   skiing at a resort   the best movie   late for class
   the winning ticket**

   _____

   _____

   _____

   _____

 Rewrite one of your older pieces of writing, adding adjective and adverb phrases.

Usage

Subjects and verbs need to agree **in number**: singular subjects take singular verbs; plural subjects take plural verbs.

1. Circle the correct **verb** in parentheses for each sentence.

   (a) The students (is, are) going to the assembly.

   (b) A black dog (runs, run) by this corner every day.

   (c) The jet (need, needs) refueling every twelve hours.

   (d) Underwater caves (is, are) fascinating to explore.

   (e) They (was, were) repaving our street today.

2. Proofread this paragraph for **subject-verb agreement**. Rewrite it, fixing any verbs that do not agree with their subjects.

   The team are exhausted after the game. Penalties were given regularly in every period. Rachel, the coach, complain to the referee whenever she can. It are no use. The game are over and we waits for the next one to be played.

   _____

   _____

   _____

   _____

   _____

   _____

   _____

   _____

   _____

Here are some **subject-verb agreement** tips.

- Make compound subjects joined by **and** take a plural verb.

  The horse and rider **jump** the fence.

- Compound subjects joined by **or** or **nor**: make the verb agree with the part of the subject near the verb.

  Ten words or **one sentence is** all that you need.

- Collective nouns, such as **team**, **jury**, **class**, and **committee** take the singular verb.

  The committee **is** considering your proposal.

Design an ad! Your rough copy is given below. Rewrite it, fixing subject-verb agreement problems. Draw or add pictures to make the ad stand out.

> This is the rough copy for the ad.

A Revolutionary New Shoe!

You needs it! You wants it!
It are the new, revolutionary
Walk THIS!
This are the shoe with an attitude.
Wears it to the show!
Shows it to your friends!
See how they wants to has their own pair, just like you!
Walk THIS!
The shoe with the attitude!
Makes it your attitude NOW!

> This is where your good copy for the ad is written. Add your pictures or drawings below.

▶▶ *Illustrate your ad with an eye-catching design.*

Usage Problems

Sentence Fragments

When writing, make sure you use full sentences.

My dog eats toast with us in the morning, whenever he has the chance.

NOT: Whenever he has the chance.

> A **sentence fragment** is a group of words that doesn't express a complete thought. A sentence expresses a complete thought.

1. Check the following for **sentence fragments**. Rewrite any sentence fragments on the lines. Add words to make them complete sentences.

   (a) The gigantic bubble burst over the crowd.

   (b) Showering them with droplets of water.

   (c) Rushed out of the stands.

   (d) Others calmly raised their umbrellas.

   (e) Whenever it rains.

   _____

   _____

   _____

   _____

2. Sometimes **sentence fragments** can be used, such as

   • in advertisements: **"The colour! The texture! The cost!"**

   • in conversational language: **"Hey!" "So, what?"**

   (a) Write advertisement copy for one of these products. Use **sentence fragments** in some of your copy.

   a new toothbrush   **car-wash soap**   **game software**   **foot powder**   **a new singer**

   _____

   _____

   _____

   _____

   (b) Add to this conversation using mostly **sentence fragments**.
   "Hey!"
   "What?"

   _____

   _____

   _____

   _____

▶▶ *Write a poem on a topic of your choice. Use only sentence fragments.*

In your writing, watch for **run-on sentences**. A run-on sentence goes past its "natural" stopping point. For example, read how this sentence runs on.

> A **run-on sentence** has two or more main clauses. They're written as one sentence without conjunctions or proper punctuation.

Janine lifted the cup to her mouth she tasted the soothing herbal tea.

It is better to do one of the following:

- Janine lifted the cup to her mouth. She tasted the soothing herbal tea. (two sentences)

- Janine lifted the cup to her mouth and she tasted the soothing herbal tea. (two sentences joined by a conjunction)

- Lifting the cup to her mouth, Janine tasted the soothing herbal tea. (creating an absolute phrase; rewording as necessary)

- Janine lifted the cup to her mouth; she tasted the soothing herbal tea. (using a semicolon to join two simple sentences)

1. Using the above methods as a guide, rewrite these **run-on sentences** so that they read properly.

   (a) The plane climbed higher into the clouds its engines sputtered as the storm increased.

   _____

   _____

   (b) Our final day this term was fun a party was planned and we went to it in the cafeteria.

   _____

   _____

   (c) The car skidded on the ice pieces of hardened snow swept off into the other lane.

   _____

   _____

2. Read this **run-on sentence**. Rewrite it, separating it into sentences that make sense. Vary the methods you use.

   Carol had wanted tickets to the game so badly she had called every agency no one seemed to have any extras there were still seats left it was possible she might be able to purchase a cancelled one if only it was true.

   _____

   _____

   _____

   _____

   _____

   _____

Find examples of run-on sentences in everyday writing. Rewrite them using the suggestions above.

Usage Problems

In your writing, make sure not to have **comma splices**. For example, Manon ran to the gate, she made it through.

> A **comma splice** links two main clauses. It is incorrect usage, similar to a run-on sentence.

It is better to do one of the following:

- Manon ran to the gate. She made it through.
- Manon ran to the gate and she made it through.
- As Manon ran to the gate, she made it through.

1. Using conjunctions, fix these **comma-splice sentences**.

    (a) Harry jumped into his car, he sped away.

    _____

    (b) The time for action is now, we must not give up!

    _____

    (c) My pet python loves me, it gives me a big hug every day.

    _____

2. Rewrite and correct these **comma-splice sentences**.

    (a) L'Anse Aux Meadows is located at the northern tip of Newfoundland, the Vikings landed there.

    _____

    _____

    (b) Children played for years among the ruins of Viking homes, it was not even suspected.

    _____

    (c) Today it is an international historic site, they have rebuilt the settlement.

    _____

    _____

3. Using **subordinate clauses**, fix these **comma-splice sentences**. You may have to reword parts of the sentences.

    (a) The train pulled into the station, passengers disembarked onto the platform.

    _____

    _____

    (b) Skiers flew down the hill, trees were dodged at high speed.

    _____

    _____

 Read through newspaper copy or other material for comma splices. Share them.

1. What is the difference between a **common noun** and a **proper noun**?

   _____

2. Give the **plural** form for each of these nouns.

   calf: _____   child: _____

   man: _____   box: _____

   dish: _____   sheep: _____

3. What is an **antecedent**? _____

4. Write a **pronoun** for each noun.

   Jeanette: _____   city: _____

   women: _____   Marion's: _____

   Derek: _____   car's: _____

5. For this sentence, write down the **pronouns** and **the words they refer to**.

   That evening, Patrick left the building, yet he knew it would never let him back in.

   _____

6. What is the difference between the **active** and **passive voice** of verbs?

   _____

7. Identify each sentence as using the **active** or **passive voice**.

   (a) The rain pelted down on the road. _____

   (b) Workers were drenched in the downpour. _____

   (c) Trucks were dispatched to the rescue. _____

   (d) Flood waters crashed through the town. _____

   (e) Everybody cheered when the rains stopped. _____

8. Complete this **verb tense** chart.

Present	Past	Future
happen	_____	_____
_____	found	_____
remember	_____	_____
_____	_____	will be

   Now, use one of the verbs from the chart in a sentence.

   _____

Parts of Speech 2

1. What is a **conjunction**? _____
   _____

2. Make a list of at least five **conjunctions**. _____
   _____

   Now, use one of your conjunctions to rewrite these sentences as a **compound sentence**.
   The winter was long and cold. We waited anxiously for spring.

   _____

3. What is a **preposition**? _____
   _____

4. Make a list of at least five **prepositions**. _____
   _____

5. Use **prepositions** to complete the phrases in these sentences.

   (a) The driver _____ the car sped away _____ the scene.

   (b) Many stories _____ the last century keep turning up _____ new textbooks.

   (c) I wanted to try climbing but the thought of falling prevented me _____ trying.

6. What is an **interjection**? _____
   _____

7. Add **interjections** to these sentences.

   (a) _____ Where is the pizza dough?

   (b) _____ You thought this might work.

   (c) _____ I can't hear the speaker!

   (d) _____ I think we can win.

   (e) _____ Will you please learn your lines?

8. Write three sentences: one that uses a **conjunction**; one that uses a **preposition**; and one that uses an **interjection**.

   (a) _____
   _____

   (b) _____
   _____

   (c) _____
   _____

1. What are the **four kinds of sentences**? (HINT: Each has a different purpose.)

   _____, _____, _____, _____

2. Write one example of **each kind of sentence** listed in Activity #1.

   (a) _____

   _____

   (b) _____

   _____

   (c) _____

   _____

   (d) _____

   _____

3. Use **end punctuation** to create different purposes for these same sentences.

   I have an exam today____   I have an exam today____   I have an exam today___

4. Complete this statement: **A simple sentence has a** _____ **and a** _____.

5. In each sentence, underline the **complete subject**. Circle the **complete predicate**.
   (a) The small boat drifted out into the bay.
   (b) Thirty cyclists competed in the race.
   (c) An extremely hot lump of coal landed in Durell's coffee.
   (d) Mitch found the test very difficult to finish.
   (e) The older building crumbled to the ground in a whoosh of smoke.

6. Write five **simple sentences.** Underline the **subject** in each. Circle the **predicate** in each.

   (a) _____

   _____

   (b) _____

   _____

   (c) _____

   _____

   (d) _____

   _____

   (e) _____

   _____

1. Describe a **compound sentence**. _____

   _____

2. Make a **compound sentence** out of each pair of **simple sentences**.

   (a) The climbers reached the summit. They cheered wildly.

   _____

   (b) Our descent has been planned. We must be careful.

   _____

3. Describe a **complex sentence**. _____

   _____

4. Add main **simple sentences** to these to make **complex sentences**.

   (a) After reaching the mountain's base, _____

   (b) Although the climbing team was exhausted, _____

5. Write a **compound sentence**, then a **complex sentence**. You may wish them to deal with the same content.

   (a) _____

   _____

   (b) _____

   _____

6. What is the difference between a **direct object** and an **indirect object**?

   _____

7. Write a sentence with a **direct object**. Underline the **object**.

   _____

8. Write a sentence with an **indirect object**. Underline the **indirect object**.

   _____

9. Underline the **subject complement** in each sentence.

   (a) The car smells new.   (b) The brakes are worn.

10. Write a sentence with a **subject complement**. Underline the **subject complement**.

   _____

   _____

CHECK UP 3 Clauses

1. What is the difference between a **main clause** and a **subordinate clause**?

   _____

2. Add a **subordinate clause** to each **main clause**.

   (a) The train pulled into the station _____

   _____

   (b) _____ the passengers got
        on board.

   (c) Hours passed _____

   _____

   (d) _____ the train arrived at the
        terminal.

   (e) _____ their vacation could begin.

3. Add a **main clause** to each **subordinate clause**.

   (a) _____ after the train
        had stopped.

   (b) While we sat waiting for the taxi, _____

   _____

   (c) Although the train seats were comfortable, _____

   _____

   (d) _____ while our bags were checked.

   (e) When we saw the taxi, _____

   _____

4. Write five sentences. Use **main** and **subordinate clauses** in each sentence.

   (a) _____

   _____

   (b) _____

   _____

   (c) _____

   _____

   (d) _____

   _____

   (e) _____

   _____

78

CHECK UP 4 ▸ *Subject-Verb Agreement*

1. Complete this statement: **Singular subjects need _____ verbs;**

   plural subjects need _____ verbs.

2. Circle the **correct verb** in parentheses for each sentence.

   (a) The concert (is, are) going on as scheduled.

   (b) Five thousand tickets (was sold, were sold) this week alone!

   (c) The lead singer (has, have) a link to the city.

   (d) He (was, were) born here twenty years ago.

   (e) Everyone (hope, hopes) the music (live, lives) up to its hype.

3. Check this paragraph written in the present tense for **subject-verb agreement**. Rewrite the corrected paragraph.

   We is so overwhelmed! The limo stop right by us, and Frail, the lead singer, steps out. He greet us with a smile, calls the rest of the band, and they walks into the crowd. We is walking with them as we speak! Frail have just turned around.
   "Do you want a tour of the stage?" he ask. We runs past him to the stage door. Well, wouldn't you?

   _____

   _____

   _____

   _____

   _____

   _____

   _____

   Now, write a paragraph that tells about the tour of the stage. Use proper **subject-verb agreement**.

   _____

   _____

   _____

   _____

   _____

   _____

CHECK UP 5 ▸ *Usage Problems*

1. Put a check mark beside each **sentence fragment**.

   (a) Ran to the water fountain. _____

   (b) We caught the excitement. _____

   (c) The car just missed the sign post. _____

   (d) Thirty people at the storefront. _____

   (e) Into the endless abyss. _____

2. Rewrite and correct these **run-on sentences**.

   (a) The crowd broke up at noon it reassembled two blocks away.

   _____

   (b) Police were called in it looked as if the situation could escalate.

   _____

   (c) Cheers were heard up and down the street two cars pulled up to the curb.

   _____

   (d) A hush settled the actress stepped from the car her hand was raised to the onlookers.

   _____

   (e) She moved with elegance her face beamed a smile the crowd went silent.

   _____

3. Rewrite and correct these sentences containing **comma splices**.

   (a) Julia found her bracelet, it was under a couch pillow.

   _____

   (b) The bracelet had been given to her when she was ten, her aunt sent it to Julia as a present.

   _____

   (c) Promptly, she lost it again, this time it seemed gone for good.

   _____

   (d) Julia had an idea, she checked her mom's wrist.

   _____

   (e) It turned out that Julia's mother wore it to a dance, she had forgotten to return it, the two decided to share the bracelet from now on.

   _____

   _____

Unit 4

Putting It Together!

FOCUS ON: Creative Writing

Think about your own **writing** as you answer these questions.

It's a good idea to think about what you like in **creative writing**. This helps organize your thoughts as you think about what to write.

1. What **topics** do you find the most interesting to write about?

   _____

   _____

2. What **form** do you prefer to write (such as poem, short story, or journal entry)?

   _____

3. What are some **reasons** why you write? _____

   _____

Think about **writing** in general as you answer these questions.

1. What are some differences between a **poem** and **prose writing** (such as a short story)?

   _____

   _____

   _____

   _____

2. What are the steps in the **writing process**?

   _____

   _____

3. List some types of **media writing**.

   _____

   _____

   _____

   _____

4. What is a **paragraph**? _____

   _____

5. What is an **essay**? _____

   _____

6. Describe the concept of **audience** in writing. _____

   _____

   _____

 Describe your favourite piece of either your own or someone else's writing. What makes this piece your favourite?

Putting It Together!　*The Writing Process*

There are some basic steps to follow in the writing process:

- **predrafting:** getting ideas about your writing; planning your thoughts;

- **drafting:** putting your ideas down for the first time;

- **revising:** going over your writing; possibly rethinking what you have written, and changing some of the ideas;

- **editing/proofreading:** checking your writing for errors and continuity of content—you could have a friend check your work at this stage;

- **publishing:** sharing your writing with others in a final, polished form.

1. Select one of the following writing ideas. Use the **predrafting** step to get some ideas about how to approach the writing. For example, would you write a poem? a story? a piece of non-fiction?

    going to a concert　　**playing on a team**　　**a funny experience**　　**a scary moment**
    a date

    _____

    _____

    _____

    _____

    _____

2. Use the **drafting** step to create a rough draft of the writing idea you selected in Activity #1. Make your draft fit on this page.

    _____

    _____

    _____

    _____

    _____

    _____

    _____

    _____

    _____

    _____

 Take your writing to the next step in the writing process. When you feel it is good enough to share with a friend, even though it is still a rough draft, do so to get some feedback.

Putting It Together!

One of the most difficult parts of writing is getting an idea of what to write about.

> Good ideas come from many sources. Think of this: Most writers agree that you should write about what you know.

Here are some tips on how to come up with an idea.

- Talk with friends about story ideas.
- Go over past experiences, or dreams you've had recently.
- Think about "What if?" situations.
- Write freely on any subject that you are interested in.
- Read stories or other writings that interest you. This often gives you ideas.
- Review some of your older writing. You may want to continue an idea.
- Jot down ideas as they come into your head. Some writers keep pads of paper with them so they can write down ideas as they think of them.

1. What **method** do you use to generate ideas? _____

_____

2. One method of generating ideas is to **brainstorm** a topic by yourself or with a friend.

> Brainstorming is a good way to generate many ideas without having to worry about which is the right one.

Select one of these story titles. Brainstorm ideas that could be generated from the title. Think of characters, setting, plot ideas, anything that you think would add to the writing.

Words of Wisdom   **Driving Down the Highway**   **A Loose Thread**
The Final Product   **From Saturn**

_____

_____

_____

_____

_____

3. Another way of generating ideas is to create a **web**. A web is similar to brainstorming, although you write your ideas as if attached to a central theme or idea. Create a web of brainstormed ideas for the following topic.

> A web uses speech balloons or lines. All words or ideas are connected to the central idea.

The Last Answer

 Use one of the ideas you generated to start a story or poem.

Putting It Together! *Gathering Information*

Writers often gather information from many **sources**.
Here are a few tips.

Gathering information is part of the planning or predrafting stage. If you gather information before writing, it will make your writing more creative and *real*.

- Read newspapers and magazines for information.
- Talk to friends and teachers to get ideas to use in your writing.
- Use the Internet to look up information on a variety of topics.
- For characterization, observe how people behave and react toward each other.
- Observe your own neighbourhood to get ideas on how people live in families.
- Watch television critically to get ideas for what characters might do in real and made-up situations.

1. List some ways you would gather **information** for stories based on these ideas.

    (a) a story about a mountain climber: _____

    _____

    (b) a story about a dentist: _____

    _____

    (c) a story about an ancient Egyptian Pharaoh: _____

    _____

    (d) a true story about a medical breakthrough: _____

    _____

    (e) a poem about the sinking of the *Titanic*: _____

    _____

2. Select one of the ideas from Activity #1. **Research** the information using the methods indicated, and list some of the ideas on the lines.

    _____

    _____

    _____

    _____

    _____

3. Write some things you feel are important to know when creating a **character** for a story (for example, the character's height, age, hair colour, eye colour, likes/dislikes). What else?

    _____

    _____

    _____

    _____

 Create a character using the descriptive ideas you listed in Activity #3.

Putting It Together!   *Selecting an Audience*

All writers think of their **audience** when they write. Knowing who will read their stories or poems helps them write works that are suited to the readers.

> An audience is the reader of the writing or the observer of what is happening. Writing without an audience—even if the audience is just the writer—has little or no purpose.

1. Indicate who you think the **audience** might be for each of the following:

    (a) a story about a child in Grade 2: _____

    (b) a financial report on the stock market: _____

    (c) a review of the latest CD by a heavy metal band: _____

    (d) an article on a hockey game between the Leafs and the Canadiens: _____

    (e) a poem about the newness of spring: _____

    (f) an exam on the term's work in English: _____

    (g) a mathematics textbook for Grade 12 students: _____

    (h) a story about drug use on the streets of Toronto: _____

    (i) an article on snowboarding in Banff: _____

    (j) a report on the building codes in a particular city: _____

2. Indicate what **type** or **types of writing** might interest each of these audiences.

    (a) a banker: _____

    (b) a Grade 9 student: _____

    (c) a teacher of Science: _____

    (d) a taxi driver: _____

    (e) an airline pilot: _____

3. You are a reader. What **types of writing** interest you? List some.

    _____

    _____

    _____

    _____

    _____

4. Select a **topic** to write about. Indicate the **audience** you would write for, and whether you would write **fiction** or **non-fiction**. Explain your choice of audience.

    _____

    _____

    _____

    _____

 Read something that you feel excludes you from its audience. What happens when the audience is out of sync with the writing?

Putting It Together! *Paragraphs: Characteristics*

Paragraphs have three characteristics:

- **unity**: This means the paragraph contains only what is important or relevant to the topic.

- **coherence**: This means the paragraph has a logical progression of ideas.

- **emphasis**: This means the paragraph's important elements are emphasized or stand out.

Paragraphs have two main sentences: the **topic sentence** expresses the main idea of the paragraph, while the **clinching sentence** ends the paragraph and sums up what was happening.

1. Here is a **topic sentence** for a paragraph on dog training: **Dogs trained as puppies turn out to be the best pets in the home**. Write a topic sentence for each of these paragraph ideas.

    (a) making a lunch: _____

    _____

    (b) selecting a video: _____

    _____

    (c) organizing a Saturday night party: _____

    _____

    (d) studying for a driver's license: _____

    _____

    (e) selecting an essay topic: _____

    _____

2. Here are the **topic** and **clinching sentences** for a paragraph on dog training:

    Topic Sentence: Dogs trained as puppies turn out to be the best pets in the home.

    Clinching Sentence: They will always remain loyal to the family that cares for them.

    Write two or three **linking sentences** that complete the paragraph, linking the topic sentence to the clinching sentence.

    _____

    _____

    _____

    _____

    _____

    _____

    _____

▶▶ *Write a paragraph on one of the topics from Activity #1. Use effective sentences to make your paragraph interesting.*

Putting It Together! *Paragraphs: Narrative*

A **narrative paragraph** is a story told by a narrator, who might use the first or third person.

> Narrative paragraphs are used to tell the story. When writing narrative, be sure to include details which make your story real and vivid for the reader. Remember to involve the five senses in your details.

Here is an example of a narrative paragraph.

The ship heaved in the waves, crashing from one wall of water into the next. Crew members, frightened for their lives, had scurried below into cabins, hoping for a miracle from the dread of the storm. The captain called out for all hands to take their stations, but to no avail. The gale-force winds had the ship in its grip, and doom lurked in the spray lashing at the vessel.

1. Continue the narrative of the ship by writing the **next narrative paragraph**, saying what you think happens next.

   _____

   _____

   _____

   _____

   _____

   _____

   _____

   _____

   _____

2. Select one of these topics and write a **narrative paragraph** of at least four sentences on it.

   lost in the mountains   **a summer's day at the beach**
   winning the race   **playing guitar in a band**
   finding a wallet   **the tornado**
   buying a new stereo   **first driving lesson**

   _____

   _____

   _____

   _____

   _____

   _____

   _____

   _____

   _____

 Write a short story that uses only narrative paragraphs.

Putting It Together! *Paragraphs: Expository*

An **expository paragraph** presents information about a topic. Its purpose is to inform, explain, and even to persuade.

> An expository paragraph might explain, define, classify, identify, illustrate, compare or contrast, and analyse.

Here is an example of an expository paragraph.

In the beehive, the queen's chamber is a place of endless activity. Eggs laid by the queen are taken to cells made out of wax. Here, the workers will tend them until they hatch into larvae. When the larvae mature, they will take their place among the rest of the hive, working hard to keep the bee community alive and healthy.

1. Write an **expository paragraph** explaining what you do when you get up in the morning.

   _____

   _____

   _____

   _____

   _____

   _____

   _____

   _____

   _____

2. Another type of **expository paragraph** is the "how to" kind, where the writer explains *how* to do something. Write an **expository "how to" paragraph** on making a great sandwich.

   _____

   _____

   _____

   _____

   _____

   _____

   _____

   _____

   _____

   _____

   _____

   _____

 Read through newspapers or magazines, collecting examples of expository paragraphs. Describe what you feel makes the better ones "successful."

Putting It Together! *Essay: Thesis Statement*

A **thesis statement** in an essay is a statement that gives the writer's point of view clearly and concisely. It is usually found at the beginning of the essay.

Here is a thesis statement for an essay on **bear traps**:

The use of bear traps by hunters is an inhumane and terrible way to capture bears.

What point of view is the writer taking with this thesis statement?

_____

> An **essay** is a piece of writing that allows the writer to express a point of view. It has three sections:
> - **introduction**, which includes the thesis statement
> - **body**, which includes the main section of the essay
> - **conclusion**, which summarizes the main point of the essay, and presents the writer's final thoughts or opinion.
>
> A point of view is the opinion or approach the writer takes in examining the subject.

1. Underline the most effective thesis statement for an essay on the dangers of car racing.

    (a) Car racers need to be careful.

    (b) A racing car is a fast machine!

    (c) Race car driving can be exhilarating, but the dangers can outweigh the excitement.

    (d) A day at the races is fun, but dangerous.

    Give a reason for your choice of thesis statement.

    > Think:
    > - Was the point of view clear and concise?
    > - Did the writer state the thesis in an easily understandable way?

    _____

    _____

2. Write a concise and clear **thesis statement** on the topic of concert ticket prices. Make sure that your thesis statement clearly shows your opinion.

3. Select one of these topics. Write a **thesis statement** that clearly shows your opinion.

    homework over the holidays   **job interviews**
    pressure on teenagers   **TV sitcoms**

    _____

    _____

    _____

    _____

4. Select an **essay topic** related to a piece you have read in class. Write down what the topic is, then write a **thesis statement** that clearly shows your opinion.

    Topic: _____

    Thesis Statement: _____

    _____

 Read through an essay. Describe in your own words what the thesis statement is.

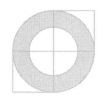

Putting It Together! *Essay: Introduction and Body*

A good **introduction** to an essay gets the reader's attention quickly. The thesis statement should set the tone of the essay. Here is an introduction to an essay on **bear traps**:

> The introduction and the body of the essay are made up of paragraphs. Each paragraph should:
> • have **unity of thought**;
> • have **coherent, clearly organized ideas**;
> • **emphasize the ideas presented**.

The use of bear traps is an inhumane and terrible way to capture bears. Their use should be questioned by all people. We need to look at the reasons why they still are part of the hunter's equipment.

1. Write your own **introduction** to an essay on graduated licensing. Make your introduction about four or five sentences long.

   _____

   _____

   _____

   _____

   _____

A good **body** of an essay develops the ideas presented in the introduction. Comparisons are made. The writer often gives reasons, pro and con, looking at both sides of the essay topic.

Facts and evidence, where necessary, are given to support the point of view. The writer leads to a natural **conclusion** where a solution is presented.

2. Continue developing the **essay topic** on graduated licensing. What are some facts, evidence, or other ideas you would put in the **body** of the essay to support your point of view?

   _____

   _____

   _____

   _____

   _____

   _____

   _____

   _____

   _____

   _____

 Read through an essay. Tell what ideas the author used in the body of the essay to present his/her point of view.

Putting It Together! *Essay: Conclusion*

The **conclusion** of an essay should be short and to the point. Conclusions of short essays do not need to summarize the essay's main points. Here is a conclusion for an essay on **bear traps**:

> Longer essays of many pages and points should contain a summary of the main points presented in the body. When starting your opinion, avoid the use of the first person (I). The reader should be able to understand your point of view by reading what you have put on paper.

Bear traps have been found to be extremely harmful to the animals. All the evidence points to the conclusion that they should not be used, no matter what the reason. Until there is an outright ban on their use, too many bears will suffer needlessly and many will die horrible, unnecessary deaths.

1. Write your own **conclusion** to the graduated licensing essay. Make your conclusion at least three or four sentences long.

    _____
    _____
    _____
    _____
    _____
    _____

2. Select an essay topic of your choice. Write a **thesis statement** that clearly shows your point of view. List items you would include in the **body** of the essay to support your thesis statement. Write a possible **conclusion** of three or four sentences to end your essay.

    Thesis Statement: _____
    _____

    Body: _____
    _____
    _____
    _____

    Conclusion: _____
    _____
    _____
    _____
    _____
    _____
    _____
    _____

 Read through an essay. Tell why you think its conclusion was effective or not.

Putting It Together!

An **editorial** is an opinion piece that usually appears in a newspaper or magazine.

TV commentators often present editorials based on a news item of the day.

> A good editorial should draw the reader to its point of view. It should be well written, and formal in tone. It should also limit the use of "I."

This form of opinion writing is similar to an essay, but is often presented in the first person (I). It takes a particular point of view, and can be very personal in tone. Here is part of an editorial on licensing cats:

Compulsory dog licensing follows a long-standing community tradition. No one disputes that dog owners should tag their pets. Yet, it's practically impossible to convince cat lovers that *their* pets should be licensed also. We feel this is an injustice to our other four-legged constituents and shouldn't be tolerated.

What point of view does this **editorial** seem to be taking on the subject of cat licensing?

_____

_____

1. Complete the above **editorial** in your own words, advocating the opinion it has expressed so far. Use three or four sentences to write the rest of the editorial.

    _____

    _____

    _____

    _____

    _____

2. Select one of these topics. Write a short **editorial** that expresses your point of view. You could write as if you were editor of a newspaper, or adopt a more personal tone.

    school rules   **smoking in restaurants**   **violence in hockey**   **musical tastes**

    _____

    _____

    > Avoid using sensational language in your editorial. Get the reader to agree with you through your emphasis of the issue. A short editorial that states the problem concisely and presents an opinion in an interesting fashion will be read with more enthusiasm than a longer, drawn-out one.

    _____

    _____

    _____

    _____

    _____

    _____

    _____

 Collect some editorials that you feel effectively get their point across. Tell why you think they are effective.

A **letter to the editor** is a pure opinion piece. It is written in the first person (I) and expresses a particular opinion on a topic of the day. Letters to the editor often take a pro or con stance. The writers usually present their opinions quite strongly. Here is a letter to the editor on the issue of cat licensing:

> Letters to the editor, while presenting opinions, should not resort to foul or threatening language. Such letters will be disregarded and not used by the editor.

Dear Editor,

    Your editorial of Wednesday was way out of line! I have three cats that stay indoors all the time. They have been declawed and pose no threat to anyone. Why should I have to have my cats licensed if they never set foot out of the house? What harm are they doing?

    The next time you want to present an argument of this nature, you might consider talking to cat owners and getting their opinions first. Shoddy reporting is no excuse for sloppy opinion writing.

Sincerely,
A. Milner,
Winnipeg

1. Write a **letter to the editor** that presents a different view from that of A. Milner. Make your letter at least four or five sentences long.

   _____

   _____

   _____

   _____

   _____

   _____

   _____

2. Select a topic that is a current issue. Write a **letter to the editor** expressing your views.

   _____

   _____

   _____

   > A current issue can usually be found in the local newspaper. Look on the Editorial page to get some ideas from other letter writers.

   _____

   _____

   _____

   _____

 Select from your local newspaper a letter to the editor that you disagree with. Write your own letter, expressing a different view. You might consider actually sending the letter!

Putting It Together!

Speech

A **speech** is a great way to share your ideas. Speeches can be **impromptu** (casual, without much preparation) or **formal** (a prepared speech, usually given for a set amount of time).

A formal speech has
- an **introduction**: needs to "grab" the audience; contains the central focus of your speech
- a **body**: the main part of your speech, usually broken into four to six paragraphs
- a **conclusion**: the wrap-up part where you tie everything together.

> Speeches can be made whenever you talk in public. P.A. announcements are a form of speech, as are anecdotes or short stories. Even telling a good joke is a form of speech. A speech involves you, the speaker, talking on a subject to a group of people who form an audience. It's really a way to get your ideas across.

Here is an example of an introduction to a speech on global warming:

For over three centuries, we have been pouring ever-increasing amounts of carbon dioxide into the atmosphere. Just now we are beginning to realize the potential danger of this. What can we do to prevent all-out global warming in the coming decades?

Use this space to prepare a **speech** of your own.

1. What do you want to talk about? Write down some **topics** you find interesting. Keep them specific. Select the one you feel could make a good speech.

   _____

   _____

   _____

2. What are some things you need to include in your speech? These are the details that would make up the **body of the speech**. Also include where you may need to go to get information, such as the library.

   _____

   _____

   _____

   _____

   _____

3. How would you **conclude** your speech? Include any wrap-up ideas you feel are needed.

   _____

   _____

4. Write a **sample opening line** or **lines** to your speech. Make sure the opening can grab your audience's attention.

   _____

   _____

▶▶ *Prepare your speech, then deliver it to a group.*

Putting It Together! *Debate*

A **debate** is a method for looking at both sides of an issue. It usually involves at least two speakers who present **arguments** that support each point of view. Debates follow specific rules and often have time limits for each speaker. Some key speech concepts are:

A debate can be formal or informal. It can involve a whole group adding ideas and arguments to the issue. True debating skill lies in being able to convince the audience that your point of view is correct. The side that convinces the audience wins the debate.

- **resolution**: the issue presented as a statement to be debated;

- **affirmative side**: the side or speaker arguing "for" the resolution;

- **negative side**: the side or speaker arguing "against" the resolution;

- **definition**: the key ideas as presented by the affirmative side. These are rebutted (argued against) by the opposing side.

- **case**: the stand that each side takes in the debate. The goal of each side is to convince the audience that its case is correct.

- **rebuttal**: opposing the ideas presented by the other side by giving differing views.

1. Plan a debate! Here is an example of a **resolution**:
   Be it resolved that smoking on school property by any individual not be allowed during regular school hours.
   Write a resolution of your own that you think would be a good debatable topic.

   _____

   _____

   _____

2. Decide which side you would take for your debate: **affirmative** or **negative**. Write some ideas that would support your point of view.

   _____

   _____

   _____

   _____

   _____

   _____

3. Think about the opposing side. What might be some of the arguments presented that you may have to rebut?

   _____

   _____

   _____

4. Plan your **debate**. This could be done individually or as a team. Work out your arguments with supporting facts where necessary. Good luck!

 Present a debate in front of the class. Try to convince the audience of your position.

Putting It Together!

Descriptive Writing

Descriptive writing can have two purposes: to be **informative** or to be **imaginative**.

> Descriptive writing is found in many forms: recipes, manuals, guide books, etc. Good descriptive writing should be able to create vivid images in your mind.

- **informative**: uses clear, specific details, such as size, shape, colour, texture, time, how something is made, or what sound something makes. Look at this example:

  The tree that was cut down last night was an old oak, probably over two hundred years in age. Its bark had cracked due to disease and its falling branches had become a danger to passing vehicles.

- **imaginative**: uses imaginative language to create images in the reader's mind; creates an overall mood or atmosphere in the writing. Look at this example:

  The stars danced in the sky, glistening and shimmering over the city. These sparkling lights from distant reaches of space glowed faintly above the heads of people unaware of the brilliance.

1. Write an **informative descriptive paragraph** of four or five sentences on a topic of your choice.

   _____

   _____

   _____

   _____

   _____

   _____

   _____

   _____

   _____

2. Write an **imaginative descriptive paragraph** of four or five sentences on a topic of your choice.

   _____

   _____

   _____

   _____

   _____

   _____

   _____

   _____

   _____

   _____

 Reread your descriptions above to see that they appeal to several senses.

Putting It Together! *Narrative Writing*

A **narrative** is a story. It is told by the speaker, or **narrator**. It can include dialogue, description, and other storytelling techniques. Look at this example.

> Many stories we read are narratives. They are always told by a storyteller, or narrator.

The cold wind bit into Kelly's face as she made her way through the snow. Only two more hours, she thought, and I'll be home. What if I'm lost? Her mind raced and she started to panic. Yet, it was her willpower and desire to be safe in the warmth of her house that drove her on. She would survive the storm.

1. Select one of these topics. Write a short **narrative** of at least four or five sentences that starts a story.

    late for school   front row at the concert   dirt-bike racing   my worst nightmare

    _____

    _____

    _____

    _____

    _____

    _____

2. List a few story ideas you would like to write about. Select one. Start a **narrative** story below. Make your narrative at least four or five sentences long.

    Your story ideas: _____

    _____

    _____

    _____

    Your narrative: _____

    _____

    _____

    _____

    _____

    _____

    _____

    _____

    _____

    _____

▶▶ *Continue the narrative you started in Activity #2 as a full story.*

Putting It Together!

Poetry

Poetry is a unique form of writing. Poems are carefully written so that the sounds of the words and the imagery (mental pictures) help convey the meaning of the writing. They can be simple or complex, a few lines or many pages. Use this page to explore your own personal poetry.

> The best way to get a feel for poetry is to read some poems. Look for a variety of poetic styles.

1. Write a "_____ ..." poem. Look at this example:

   Happiness is...
   Lying on the beach in the summer,
   Riding in a convertible,
   Eating a pizza at midnight,
   or just spending time with my friends.

   Select a topic, then write a few lines in the style of the model.

   _____

   _____

   _____

   _____

   _____

   _____

2. Write a **free verse** poem on a topic of your choice. Free verse does not follow any set rhythm. Look at this example:

   I look for meaning in this day,
   with its burning sun and dry air,
   the parched throat that constricts,
   wanting water,
   and I look for meaning
   and life.

   _____

   _____

   _____

   _____

   _____

   _____

 There are many poetic styles. Read about some of them. You may wish to try writing a poem modelled after one of the styles.

Putting It Together!

A **letter** is a way of communicating with another person on paper. There are two types of letter: **personal** and **business**. A personal letter is friendly and more informal in tone. A business letter is formal in tone. Look at these examples.

> Letters follow specific forms. Look at the examples to see how each is addressed and punctuated, and where each line starts and ends.

Business Letter

23 Main Street
Winnipeg, MN
R0G 1J6 —————————— Return address
July 12, 2000 —————————— Date

Ms. April Write —————————— Mailing address
Paper Existence Co.
P.O. Box 463
Winnipeg, MN —————————— Salutation
R0G 3P5
—————————— Body
Dear Ms. White:

   I am writing on behalf of my cousin who ordered three cartons of your paper products. They arrived two days too late for her party. I am requesting a full refund. The cartons will follow on your acceptance of my request. Thank you.

Yours truly, —————————— Complementary Closing

J. Wilson

Personal Letter

July 12, 2000

Dear Mattie,
   How are you? It was great to hear from you last week! I know it's been three months since we talked, but hey, time can't hurt our friendship. Anyway, I was hoping you could come out west this fall and visit for a few weeks. Our family would love to see you. Write back, okay? We'll set up a date. Talk to you soon!

   Sincerely,

   Louise

Write a **formal letter** replying to J. Wilson. Then write a **personal letter**, either replying to Louise or on a topic of your choice. Follow the forms of each letter as shown above.

> Notice the differences between the personal letter and the business letter.

_____   _____

_____   _____

_____   _____

_____   _____

_____   _____

_____   _____

_____   _____

_____   _____

_____   _____

_____   _____

Putting It Together!

Résumé

A **résumé** is a summary of one's experience and education. It is given to a possible employer as part of a job application. A résumé usually has these sections:

- **work experience**: an outline of previous work or volunteer experience of the applicant;
- **education**: schooling and diplomas or degrees received by the applicant;
- **skills and hobbies**: interests and other experience that the applicant has.

> A résumé should include any information that the applicant feels will help in getting the job. Skills and hobbies are important to include as the employer wants to know what the applicant's interests are. These might help in the job the applicant eventually does.

Each section tells a little more about the applicant as a person.

Complete a draft **résumé** for yourself. The information you put here could be used later in a résumé for an actual job.

WORK EXPERIENCE

> Think: baby-sitting; work done for relatives; paper routes; summer initiatives such as lawnmowing; winter initiatives such as driveway snow-shovelling; volunteer experience, and so on. List these beginning with the most recent, and going back in time.

EDUCATION

> Think: schools attended; courses taken outside of school; leadership, scout and guide camps; training outside of regular schooling, such as music lessons, martial arts classes; and so on. List these starting from the most recent, and going back in time.

SKILLS AND HOBBIES

> Think: hobbies that you have had; games you enjoy playing; clubs you have belonged to; other interests you have; and so on. List these in any order.

 Create a résumé for yourself on a computer. Include scanned-in pictures and different fonts or typefaces to make your résumé attractive.

Putting It Together!

Advertising Copy

Advertisements are written to sell something. Ad writers take great care to make the products they are trying to sell sound desirable. Read these two lines advertising a used car for sale:

> Advertisements can range from a yard sale announcement to the larger ad campaigns to sell any number of products. Their main goal is to convince the reader that what they are selling (or describing) is desirable, or wanted by the reader.

(a) Selling a car to the best buyer; used for a while; willing to negotiate price.

(b) Nearly new Mustang in mint condition for sale; willing to negotiate the price for the interested buyer!

Which ad line do you think is more effective? Give reasons for your answer.

_____

_____

_____

1. Which ads that you know of are the most effective? Describe some here and give reasons for your answers.

_____

_____

_____

_____

_____

_____

2. Write an **advertisement** that tells about a garage sale at your house. Include any information you feel the reader needs to know.

> Think: time, date, items to be sold (small list), some interesting information regarding the items, and location.

_____

_____

_____

_____

3. Design an **advertisement**! Use this space to create a print ad for a product of your choice. Be as creative as possible. Include information you feel the reader needs to know.

_____

_____

_____

_____

▶▶ *Make a collection of effective ads you find in magazines, newspapers, etc.*

1. What are the steps in the **writing process**? Describe each step in a sentence.

_____

_____

_____

_____

_____

_____

2. Describe a **technique** that can be used to come up with a good story idea.

_____

_____

_____

_____

3. Why is it important to keep your **audience** in mind when you write a story?

_____

_____

_____

4. When should a story be **peer-edited**? Why?

_____

_____

_____

5. What are some other **factors** that you need to think about as you write a story (such as setting, plot, characterization)?

_____

_____

_____

_____

_____

_____

6. When is a story **ready** to be presented or "published"?

_____

_____

_____

1. An effective paragraph has three characteristics: **unity**, **coherence**, and **emphasis**. What do each of these terms mean?

   Unity: _____

   _____

   Coherence: _____

   _____

   Emphasis: _____

   _____

2. What does it mean to present the ideas in a paragraph in proper **sequence**?

   _____

   _____

3. What is the **topic sentence** of a paragraph?

   _____

   _____

4. What is a **descriptive** paragraph?

   _____

   _____

5. Write two **descriptive paragraphs** on a topic of your choice. Make your paragraphs at least four to five sentences long each.

   _____

   _____

   _____

   _____

   _____

   _____

   _____

   _____

   _____

   _____

   _____

   _____

   _____

   _____

CHECK UP 3 ▸ *Essay Writing*

1. Essays need **unity**, **coherence**, and **emphasis**. What does this mean?

   _____

   _____

2. Write a short essay on a topic of your choice. Remember that your essay needs an effective **introduction**, a **body** that supports your introduction, and an effective **conclusion**.

   _____

   _____

   _____

   _____

   _____

   _____

   _____

   _____

   _____

   _____

   _____

   _____

   _____

   _____

   _____

   _____

   _____

   _____

   _____

   _____

   _____

   _____

CHECK UP 4 ▸ *Writing for the Appropriate Audience*

1. What are some factors that need to be kept in mind when selecting an **audience** for a particular piece of writing?

    _____

    _____

2. Indicate what types of **audiences** would be appropriate for these types of writing.

    (a) a news story about the new Federal budget: _____

    (b) a nursery rhyme: _____

    (c) a story about the first alien contact: _____

    (d) an advertisement about a new luxury car: _____

    (e) an advertisement about a sale on country and western CD's: _____

    (f) a prescription from a doctor: _____

    (g) a history exam: _____

    (h) a road map: _____

    (i) a TV program description: _____

    (j) a recipe for a fudge brownie cake: _____

3. Write a short **advertisement** for a new product of your choice. Indicate who your **audience** is and write the advertisement using appropriate language and ideas.

    _____

    _____

    _____

    _____

    _____

    _____

    _____

    _____

    _____

    _____

4. Write a **TV program listing** for a television show you know. Write it for a different **audience** than it was intended for (such as a children's program listing written for an adult audience).

    _____

    _____

    _____

    _____

Unit 5

Review and Reference

Review

1. For these words, underline any **prefixes** and **suffixes**, then write the **root words**.

   (a) uninteresting: _____ (d) review: _____

   (b) overestimate: _____ (e) undivided: _____

   (c) unjustly: _____ (f) unhappiness: _____

2. For each word, write a **synonym** then an **antonym**.

   (a) heavy: _____, _____

   (b) short: _____, _____

   (c) quick: _____, _____

   (d) angry: _____, _____

   (e) polite: _____, _____

3. Use the **homonyms** in a sentence to show their meanings.

   (a) their, there: _____

   _____

   (b) night, knight: _____

   _____

   (c) flee, flea: _____

   _____

   (d) right, write: _____

   _____

   (e) flu, flew: _____

   _____

4. Rewrite these sentences that are in **colloquial English**, converting them into **standard English**.

   (a) Yeah, I cruised the highway for half a day looking for the crazy exit!

   _____

   (b) So, you got hit in the bean by the ball hit to left field, did ya?

   _____

5. Use these sports **jargon** words and terms to write a sentence or two about hockey.

   slapped   **flattened**   **rushed the net**   **flubbed the shot**

   _____

   _____

   _____

   _____

Review

1. **Similes** compare two things using "like" or "as": **We swam like fish in the sea.** Use **similes** to complete these sentences:

   (a) She ran as fast as _____

   (b) The race was like _____

   (c) We jumped the hurdles like _____

   (d) The diver flew off the board _____

   (e) He thinks _____

2. **Metaphors** add to a piece of writing by making descriptions more vivid: **The team is a herd of gazelles on the field.** Use **metaphors** to complete these sentences.

   (a) His mind is _____

   (b) The team is _____

   (c) Our final exam is _____

3. **Personification** gives human qualities to inanimate things: **The wind talked.** Use **personification** to complete these sentences.

   (a) The clouds _____

   (b) The skies _____

   (c) Many mountains _____

4. Select one of these topics. Write a sentence about the topic in **formal language**, then rewrite the sentence in **informal language**.

   selecting a TV show   watching a game   talking with a friend
   making a pizza   hiking

   (a) _____

   _____

   (b) _____

   _____

5. Write a sentence on a topic of your choice. Write it in **formal**, then **informal** language.

   (a) _____

   _____

   (b) _____

   _____

Review

1. Write down some methods you can use to help **spell** words correctly.

   _____

   _____

   _____

   _____

   _____

2. Circle the correctly spelled word in each group.

   (a) important   importent   inportant   impourtant   impertent

   (b) felxable   fluxible   flexible   flecksible   flexabble

   (c) acheive   achieve   acheeve   acheave   acheaeve

   (d) serprise   surprize   sarprise   sirprize   surprise

   (e) ceiling   cealing   ceeling   cieiling   ciiling

3. Divide these words into **syllables**. Place the accent over the **stressed syllable**.

   tomorrow: _____   yesterday: _____

   feeling: _____   happily: _____

   shipping: _____   examination: _____

4. Give the **plural** of each of these nouns.

   (a) baby: _____   (d) lamb: _____

   (b) utensil: _____   (e) octopus: _____

   (c) wolf: _____   (f) church: _____

5. Circle any misspelled words in these sentences.

   (a) The manye times that we tryed to scalle the wals were thwarted by the slimey oil running over the bricks.

   (b) Hurds of bison were comon on the prairies during the 1800's, but that changd with the westurn push for setlement.

6. Write a sentence on a topic of your choice. Read back through the sentence checking for spelling. Circle any words you think are misspelled. Check your words in a dictionary. Rewrite your sentence if necessary.

   _____

   _____

   _____

   _____

Review

1. Read these sentences. Circle any letters that should be **capitalized**.

   (a) the company moved passed dwight street on its way to the town of carlsbay.

   (b) We know the movie we want to see; we just don't know where the stanton theatre is!

   (c) cars and trucks formed a massive pile-up on hendon avenue by the wison building.

   (d) "i hope you're going to read the book *guardians of the truth* by sharon printemps," said mr. Callow, his teacher.

   (e) blaine's excuse was so lame, even hilliard didn't believe him!

2. **Capitals** are required for **proper nouns**. For example, **Toronto, Halma, Boeing 747, Chevrolet.** Make a list of ten **proper nouns**. Make sure you use capitals correctly.

   _____

   _____

   _____

3. Complete the following. Use **capital letters** where necessary.

   (a) your school's address: _____

   _____

   (b) the city, town, place where you live and the province: _____

   _____

   (c) an address of someone you know: _____

   _____

   (d) the titles of three of your favourite movies: _____

   _____

   (e) five groups or singers that you listen to: _____

   _____

4. Select your answer to Activity #3 (d) or (e). Write a short paragraph explaining one of your choices. After you have finished, check back through your paragraph for proper use of **capital letters**.

   _____

   _____

   _____

   _____

   _____

   _____

   _____

   _____

Review

1. Add the correct **end punctuation** to each of these sentences.

   (a) Why are we going this way instead of directly onto the highway____

   (b) Seventy wild horses stood quietly, watching the approach of the truck____

   (c) I can't believe I won a million dollars____

   (d) Get your net, quickly____

   (e) So, what are we to do with all of this treasure____

2. **Commas** are used to make writing clear and to give the reader a chance to pause. Read these sentences. Place **commas** in the sentences where you think they are needed.

   (a) We packed food clothing tents sleeping bags and an inflatable raft for our journey into the backwoods.

   (b) Jeremy our guide didn't think we needed to take so much for such a short hike since we were only going to be gone for three days.

   (c) Whenever we go on a hike like this we always take a little more just in case of an emergency.

   (d) Amy also a professional hiker knows the pitfalls of not taking enough supplies.

   (e) After much preparing we set out for the backwoods far from the comforts of the city.

3. **Apostrophes** are used in contractions (**can't**, **wouldn't**) and to show possession (**Mike's car**). Use **apostrophes** in (a) to make contractions. In (b), rewrite the words to show possession, using apostrophes.

   (a) I have: _____   you will: _____   she is: _____

   will not: _____   should have: _____   is not: _____

   (b) the book of Janice: _____

   the boat of Arno: _____

   the trophy of the team: _____

   the race of the ship: _____

   the flight path of the plane: _____

   the discovery of the climbers: _____

4. Write a short paragraph on a topic of your choice. Use **commas**, **apostrophes**, and correct sentence **end punctuation** in your paragraph.

   _____

   _____

   _____

   _____

   _____

   _____

Review

Read these sentences carefully. Rewrite the sentences adding **colons**, **semicolons**, **quotation marks**, **dashes**, **parentheses**, and **ellipses** where needed. (NOTE: You may want to review how these punctuation marks are used by reading the examples on pp. 34–35, 37.)

1. We carried many things tools for the car, paper, and pens two boxes of paper and a spoon.

_____

_____

2. Well, I never had to do this sighed Marcus I just wish someone had told me how to run a show

_____

_____

3. Air conditioners, fans, the garden hose all were ineffective in staving off the oppressive heat.

_____

_____

4. We tried to get Raoul it wasn't my idea to come and help us rescue the second act from disaster.

_____

_____

5. The abstract painting was well, let's just say it caused quite an uproar in the cafeteria!

_____

_____

6. Here's what you need wood, nails, a plane, a saw, and a good hammer without these things you'll never build that birdhouse.

_____

_____

7. The drummer asked When do we get a chance to see the town

_____

_____

8. The assignment due next week had two parts 1 an explanation of Canada's role in foreign affairs and 2 Canada's role in foreign aid.

_____

_____

9. Jolie's great grandfather had built the log cabin he was famous in the area for his wooden structures long before she was born.

_____

_____

10. After we win said the coach we will celebrate by visiting Clown's Circus on Main Street

_____

_____

Review

It is important to **proofread** your writing. If possible, have a friend also proofread what you write, especially if it is something you will want produced in a good copy, such as a story or an essay. Proofread for **spelling**, **punctuation**, and **capitalization**. Proofread for **proper use of words in sentences** and **proper sentence structure**.

1. Proofread these sentences for spelling, punctuation, and capitalization errors. Rewrite the sentences with corrections.

   (a) we hardly had a, chance to finnish our breakfest when; the others Attacked growled Lugen,

   _____

   _____

   (b) the Others were–simple reptilees from anothur planet in the selian sector: yet thuy had strungthbeyond that of any humman?

   _____

   _____

   (c) I know a weigh to ambush the Others? cried Wolgar we must prepar for amidnite atack;

   _____

   _____

2. Proofread these sentences for **proper sentence use of words** and **sentence structure**. Rewrite the sentences with any corrections.

   (a) Wolgar were the bravest scout in the entire company he knew what it meant to lose to the Others.

   _____

   _____

   (b) "Only those without honour would attacks at night," complained Lugen. "Your plan is not worthy of our attention."

   _____

   _____

   (c) In the night without warning Wolgar was gathering the troops the Others attacked as.

   _____

   _____

3. Write at least two more sentences to the story about Wolgar and the Others. Proofread your work for errors. Have a friend also proofread your sentences, if possible. Correct any errors that are found.

   _____

   _____

   _____

   _____

Review

1. **Nouns** name persons, places, or things. They can be **common** (city) or **proper** (Vancouver).

   For each **noun** listed, write a **common** or **proper noun** that could be paired with it.

   car: _____   movie: _____

   uncle: _____   Atlantic: _____

   Africa: _____   country: _____

2. For each boldfaced **noun** in these sentences, write a **pronoun** referring to it on the line.

   (a) **Reander** followed _____ instinct and took the taxi.

   (b) The **city** would be hit by the storm, and _____ would be snowed under for days.

   (c) _____ always knew that the time would come, but **Gibson** didn't want this to be the day.

   (d) The **boys** tried to get more signatures, but _____ survey would be incomplete.

   (e) Many **trucks** rolled along the road as _____ headed toward the mountains.

3. Verbs can be **active voice** (I **hit** the ball.) or **passive voice** (The ball **was hit** by me.). Indicate with the words **active** or **passive** what the verb is in each sentence.

   (a) The team played well today. _____

   (b) Mountains were climbed by the adventurers. _____

   (c) We drove to Thunder Bay last summer. _____

   (d) The train was delayed for two hours. _____

   (e) It rained heavily last week for three days. _____

4. Write two sentences on topics of your choice, using the **active voice** of the verb.

   (a) _____

   _____

   (b) _____

   _____

5. Write two sentences on topics of your choice, using the **passive voice** of the verb.

   (a) _____

   _____

   (b) _____

   _____

Review

1. Verbs have tenses: **present** (I **am** here.), **past** (I **was** here.), and **future** (I **will be** here.). Use the words **present**, **past**, or **future** to indicate the tense of each verb in these sentences.

   (a) The workers make materials last long into the week. _____

   (b) He was trying to rescue the dog from the parked car. _____

   (c) They will drive to Victoria in the spring. _____

   (d) We played well during the first half of the game. _____

   (e) Serena knows a great practical joke! _____

2. Each of these sentences uses the **present tense**. Rewrite the sentences in the **past tense**, then the **future tense**.

   (a) I work every summer at a part-time job.

   _____

   _____

   (b) The ship sails through the North Atlantic shipping routes.

   _____

   _____

   (c) Jason plays basketball very strangely.

   _____

   _____

   (d) Serena rides her dirt bike to school every day.

   _____

   _____

   (e) The pilot steers the plane out of disaster.

   _____

   _____

3. Interjections are words that exclaim (Ouch! Shhh!). They can stand alone or be used in sentences (**Well**, what do you say now?). Here is a partial list of interjections: **ouch**, **ugh**, **eh**, **hey**, **ah**, **ow**, **all right**, **oops**, **hey**, **hurrah**, **yeah**, **shhh**. Use some of these interjections in a short paragraph on a topic of your choice.

   _____

   _____

   _____

   _____

   _____

   _____

Review

1. A **conjunction** is a word that links two or more words or groups of words. Some conjunctions are: **and**, **but**, **or**, **nor**, **for**, **yet**, **neither**...**nor**, **either**...**or**. Complete these sentences with words added after the **boldfaced** conjunctions.

   (a) The children came into the toy store **and** _____

   _____

   (b) We liked the movie, **yet** _____

   _____

   (c) I have a great idea, **but** _____

   _____

   (d) The team won the game, **for** _____

   _____

   Now, write your own sentence using one of the **conjunctions** from above.

   _____

   _____

2. A **preposition** is a word that relates a noun or pronoun to another word in the sentence. It also starts a group of words called a **prepositional phrase**. Some prepositions are: **about**, **of**, **from**, **along**, **between**, **but**, **except**, **over**, **since**, **under**, **beside**, **toward**, and **without**. Complete these sentences with words added after the **boldfaced** prepositions.

   (a) The dog was found **beside** _____

   (b) A comet was spotted speeding **toward** _____

   (c) Our town has been **without** _____

   (d) We travelled **along** _____

   Now, write your own sentence using one of the prepositions listed above.

   _____

   _____

3. **Adjectives** and **adverbs** are describing words. They describe, or modify, nouns or pronouns (adjectives) and verbs (adverbs). In each sentence, circle the adjectives. Underline the adverbs.

   (a) The large red cabinet crashed down today.

   (b) A smaller pony galloped freely in the field.

   (c) Two ships collided in the harbour.

   Now, write two of your own sentences using adjectives and adverbs.

   _____

   _____

   _____

   _____

Review

1. There are four sentence purposes: **declarative**, **interrogative**, **exclamatory**, and **imperative**. Write the purpose of each of these sentences on the line beside it.

   (a) Come here and bring that book. _____

   (b) When did you decide to join the team? _____

   (c) I know I can do this! _____

   (d) The butterfly fluttered in and out of the bushes. _____

2. Write an example of each illustrating the four sentence purposes.

   (a) _____

   (b) _____

   (c) _____

   (d) _____

3. Two sentence types are: **simple** and **compound**. A **simple sentence** has one main clause. A **compound sentence** is made up of two simple sentences joined by a conjunction. Write the type of each of these sentences on the line beside it.

   (a) The cougar ran over the rocky hill. _____

   (b) Many antelope galloped across the plain. _____

   (c) We chased the herd but we lost them past the forest. _____

   (d) Sharon has a talent for singing, and she uses it in the school choir. _____

4. Write one example of each sentence type mentioned in Activity #3.

   (a) _____

   _____

   (b) _____

   _____

5. A sentence is made up of **clauses.** A clause is a group of words with a subject and a predicate. Only a main clause can stand alone as a sentence. Identify each of the following clauses as **main** or **subordinate**.

   (a) While the driver was waiting for the signal. _____

   (b) We started the race on time. _____

   Now, write an example of a main clause and an example of a subordinate clause.

   _____

   _____

Review

1. A **complex sentence** is made up of a main clause and one or more subordinate clauses:

   As she looked through the telescope, she saw a new comet.

   Add **main clauses** to these subordinate clauses to make complex sentences.

   (a) After diving off the board, _____

   (b) When the snow stopped falling, _____

   (c) In the middle of the test, _____

   (d) Although Petra enjoyed pizza, _____

   Add **subordinate clauses** to these main clauses to make complex sentences.

   (a) _____, the dam burst at midnight.

   (b) _____, we followed the trail.

   (c) _____, the CD was damaged.

   (d) I found my way back from the mall, _____

2. Sentences have **subjects** and **predicates**. The subject is who or what the sentence is about. The predicate is the verb, or the action that the subject does. Examine the sentence, The boy is well. **The boy** is the **subject**; **is well** is the **predicate**.

   Underline the **subject** in each sentence. Circle the **predicate** in each sentence.

   (a) The car rolled down the hill.   (d) A falling rock crashed through the window.

   (b) A crowd surged onto the stage.   (e) I listened for the sound.

   (c) We found the lost map.   (f) The injured antelope ran with the herd.

3. Subjects and verbs must agree. A singular subject takes a singular verb. A plural subject takes a plural verb. Look at these examples.

   The train arrives. (singular subject **train** with singular verb **arrives**)

   The trains arrive. (plural subject **trains** with plural verb **arrive**)

   Note that singular verbs in the present tense end with **s**; plural verbs in the present tense don't end with **s**.

   Circle the **verb** that agrees with the **subject** in each sentence.

   (a) The car (spin, spins) out of control on the ice.

   (b) Tall buildings (sway, sways) in the wind.

   (c) Forty dogs (roam, roams) freely in the back streets.

4. Write two sentences on topics of your choice. Make your **subjects** and **verbs** agree.

   _____

   _____

   _____

   _____

Review

Watch for these usage problems as you write: **sentence fragments**, **run-on sentences**, and **comma splices**.

1. Underline the **sentence fragments**. Rewrite them as complete sentences.

   (a) We had a great time at the concert.

   (b) The best way to get home.

   (c) Having spaghetti twice a day.

   (d) I don't know how I passed!

   _____

   _____

2. Read these **run-on sentences**. Rewrite them breaking them into separate sentences where necessary.

   (a) The truck gained speed on the overpass it barreled down the road at an ever-increasing speed.

   _____

   _____

   (b) A cougar stalked its prey the deer suddenly sprang to life, running away.

   _____

   _____

   (c) The wind kept the sails full we turned into the gale our craft would survive the storm.

   _____

   _____

3. Read these sentences with **comma splices**. Rewrite them as proper sentences, eliminating commas where necessary.

   (a) He never gave his money, the rest of the group had to cancel their tickets.

   _____

   _____

   (b) A fine line is drawn when arguments begin, both sides need to calm down and think.

   _____

   _____

   (c) The falling tree limb barely missed the house, grandfather hurried out of his car, he rescued his grandson just in time.

   _____

   _____

A **paragraph** is a set of sentences that expresses and supports a topic or idea. It usually has a topic sentence that sets out what the main idea is. Other sentences support the topic sentence. A paragraph ends with a good concluding sentence. Read this example.

Many radio telescopes are looking for signs of extraterrestrial life in space. They "sweep" the heavens nightly, trying to pick up any strange signal that might indicate intelligent life. Astronomers listen intently to the static sounds from deep space. One day, they may hear something that changes our view of what's out there.

1. Write a paragraph on one of the following topics. Make your paragraph at least four to five sentences long.

   **an adventure   a photograph   the wrong book
   your favourite sport   finding a wallet**

   _____

   _____

   _____

   _____

   _____

   _____

   _____

2. Write two paragraphs on a topic of your choice. Remember to make the sentences of each paragraph support the main idea of each paragraph.

   _____

   _____

   _____

   _____

   _____

   _____

   _____

   _____

   _____

   _____

   _____

Creative writing can be **prose** or **poetry**. It can be a creative letter or an essay. It may be descriptive or have dialogue. It may even be an advertisement. Each person has favourite types of writing. On this page, write a creative piece of writing using a style that you like. It can be prose or poetry in whatever form you prefer. You may wish to add a picture or design an ad to go with your writing. Be creative! Good luck!

_____

_____

_____

_____

_____

_____

_____

_____

_____

_____

_____

Editing and Proofreading Guide

All writing needs to be **edited** and **proofread**. **Editing** includes proofreading your work (checking it for errors) and making sure the words and ideas flow properly. After you finish a piece of writing, read it over to check that it makes sense. Give it to a friend to read. Ask for honest feedback. You may have to rewrite sections to make your ideas clearer to the reader.

When you **proofread**, check for errors in spelling, capitalization, punctuation, grammar, usage, and the look of the writing. The following checklist will help as you edit your work, or that of a friend.

Editing Checklist

Punctuation
✓ Have I used periods
  • at the end of each statement?
  • after abbreviations?
  • after a person's initials?
✓ Have I used question marks after questions?
✓ Have I used exclamation marks after words or sentences that show strong emotion (but not too often)?
✓ Have I used commas
  • between names and parts of addresses?
  • between parts of dates?
  • between items in a series?
  • after introductory adverbial clauses that begin a sentence but are not a vital part of it?
  • after words used in direct address ("Ravi, it is time to go.")?
  • after a subordinate clause when it begins a sentence?
  • between parts of a compound sentence?
✓ Have I used apostrophes
  • in contractions to show missing letters?
  • to show possession?
✓ Have I used quotation marks
  • to enclose a direct quotation?
  • to enclose the title of short works, such as poems, stories, and songs?
✓ Have I underlined (when handwriting) or italicized (when using a computer) book, film, and television series titles, and names of newspapers and magazines?

Capitalization
✓ Have I capitalized
  • the first word in each sentence?
  • names of people, titles when used with a name, buildings, organizations, cities, provinces, countries?
  • names of political parties, historical events, religions?
  • names of months, days of the week, holidays?
  • the pronoun "I"?

Spelling
✓ Have I used a dictionary/spell checker to confirm the spelling of those words about which I'm unsure?

Grammar
✓ Is there agreement between the subject and the verb in my sentences?
✓ Are my verb tenses consistent and correct?
✓ Have I used the correct past tense of irregular verbs?
✓ Is the person to whom each pronoun refers clear?
✓ Does each pronoun agree with its antecedent?
✓ Are subject and object forms of pronouns (who, whom) used correctly?

Usage
✓ Have frequently confused words been used correctly (red, read)?

Preparing the Manuscript
✓ Is my draft neat, double-spaced with 2.5-cm (one-inch) margins around the text?
✓ Did I indent the first line of each paragraph or double-space between my paragraphs?
✓ Do I have the page number in the upper right-hand corner of every page after the first?
✓ Does my cover sheet show the title, my name and class number, and my teacher's name?
✓ Did I proofread my paper one last time for errors?

Editing and Proofreading Guide

Use **proofreader's marks** when checking over a piece of writing. It will help the author understand what and where the errors are that need to be corrected. Use this checklist as a guide.

⋏	insert letter/word	⌃	add comma
#	insert space	⌄	add apostrophe
≡	Capital letter	ℐ	delete
/	lower case	*tr*	transpose
⌇	boldface	¶	new paragraph
⌐	new line	*stet*	Let it stand
—	set in italic type	⌄⌄	insert quotation marks
⊙	add period/other end punctuation	(*set*) ?	Insert question mark

Notice how the proofreader's marks are used in this piece of writing.

we caried the piano as far aswe could go Jason wanted to stop every two
seconds! "No way!" I said, We need to get this over to Aunt Kiris before th end
of the day," jason agreed we that had to do this, but he was getting so tired tired.
I spoke about Our promise to aunt Kiri "I know," he replied, "its been a long day.

Rewrite the corrected piece on the lines.

_____

_____

_____

_____

_____

Remember: Always edit and proofread your writing before you submit it as a final copy. Have one or more friends look it over as well.

Using Reference Materials

Reference materials are used to give us information on a variety of subjects. Two of the most useful are a **dictionary** and a **thesaurus**. A dictionary gives the spelling of a word, its meanings, part of speech, usage, and often a history (etymology) of the word. A thesaurus gives the synonyms, antonyms, and related words for a given word. Use this page to learn how to use these reference tools more effectively.

Dictionary
Dictionary entries appear in **alphabetical order.** Each dictionary page has **guide words** at the top. The first guide word tells us the first word that appears on the page; the second tells us the last word that appears on the page. For example, circle the words that would appear on a dictionary page with the guide words **safety–scruff:**

silly   skin   scream   staff   smile   sake   scythe   smart   still   scrum   scrape   sale   sail

Write some words that might appear on a dictionary page with these guide words:

land–lost

_____

_____

_____

_____

_____

_____

_____

take–trail

_____

_____

_____

_____

_____

_____

_____

Thesaurus
A thesaurus will help you find the right word for a particular context. It can help make your writing more interesting. Words in a thesaurus are usually in **alphabetical order**. To look up a word, use the guide words at the top of the pages, or look up the word in the **index** at the back of the book. A thesaurus entry will list synonyms of the given word, with any antonyms or related (similar) words that also fit. Look at this sample thesaurus entry.

HUMBLE	*adjective*	common, courteous, docile, homespun, insignificant, low, lowly, modest, obedient, polite, respectful
	antonyms	assertive, important, proud
	verb	abash, break, bring down, chasten, conquer, humiliate
	antonym	raise

Use the thesaurus to choose the word that is right for your purpose. For example, not all of the words in the above example would be suitable for every type of writing: "**He is a *humble* man**," has a slightly different meaning than "**He is a *polite* man**."

Using Reference Materials

There are many **reference sources** you can use when looking for information. Here is a list of some sources.

- **Reference Books**: Encyclopedias, almanacs, fact books, quotation books, yearbooks, and atlases can all be found in your library. They are in the Reference section, and normally can't be signed out of the library.

- **CD-ROMs**: Most of the reference material contained in books is now available on CD-ROMs. These can be found in libraries and other reference areas.

- **The Internet**: This global network lets you access information Web sites through your computer. It is an excellent way to get data fast, twenty-four hours a day.

- **Periodical Indexes**: These are listings of information found in magazines and newspapers. They are located in the reference or information sections of libraries.

- **Vertical Files**: These are collections of pictures, news clippings, brochures, and pamphlets that have been put in files and stored in filing cabinets. They are usually organized alphabetically by subject.

- **Microfilm**: This is a storage system that uses film containing the reduced images of newspapers and magazines. Special projector-like machines are used to view the microfilm.

- **Non-Print Resources**: This includes audio and videotapes, photographs, films and filmstrips, CDs, records, and so on.

- **Community Agencies**: This includes pamphlets and other material from the community, and government documents, information, and other materials. Many of these materials are available at the information and reference desks of libraries.

Information can also be gathered from people by interviews and questionnaires. This often gives the researcher first-hand knowledge of an event and can add realism to a piece of writing. Include yourself in this! Diary or journal entries are often used in writing, giving a personal touch to the piece.

List some sources, not listed on this page, you can use (or have used) to gather information.

_____

_____

_____

_____

_____

_____

Using the Internet for Research

The Internet is a global network of Web sites. It is accessed through your computer. To get connected to the Internet, you need a **modem** (cable or telephone line) and an **Internet service provider.** Once connected, you will be able to get onto the **World Wide Web.** This is a network of computers that stores **Web pages**, or Web sites. Each Web site has a Web address, usually given in this manner: **www.pearsoned.com** The three **w**'s indicate that the site is on the World Wide Web. The second part indicates the homepage (in this example Pearson Education). The **.com** indicates a company, and is the end of the address. The pages are connected to each other through **hyperlinks.** These links take you to new Web pages that usually have something in common with the site you were at. Each site could have everything from text to pictures to audio and video files. To browse the site, you click on a highlighted line, picture, or icon. You are instantly taken to that section of the site. Items at the site can be printed out or saved on your computer's hard drive.

Surfing the Web can be enjoyable, but it's better if you have an idea of what you are looking for. Use key words that can be searched for by a **search engine.** A search engine is an organizing feature of the Internet. Yahoo!, AltaVista, Google, and Lycos are examples of search engines. Load one by typing in its address (such as **www.yahoo.com**) then go to the Search box. Type in the item you are searching for, then click on **Search.** The search engine will "search" the World Wide Web for sites that match your item. It will eventually turn up **hits—sites** that have something to do with your request. Often, too many sites turn up and it's difficult to know what to look at. It's a good idea to be specific in your search. For example, if you want information on **dogs**, determine: is it a particular dog? Typing in **German Shepherd dogs** will give you more specific sites related to your search than just **dogs**.

Here is an example of a Web page from the publishing company that produced this book.

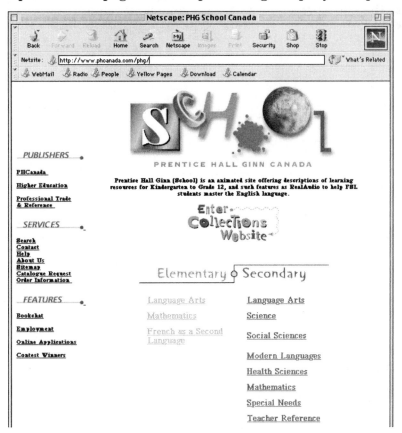

Reading Your Work Out Loud

Often, we write something, only to find that the ideas didn't quite come out right. One way to check your work is to **read it out loud**. This could include reading it to a friend or to yourself. When we hear the piece read, we often pick up things that may have seemed good in the writing but don't work in the retelling. Another reason to read your work out loud is to share it with a larger audience. Here are some things to think about when you read your work aloud.

- **Volume of voice**: Make sure your voice can be heard by all, but is not so loud that it is irritating.

- **Intonation**: This is the way you use tone of voice when you read your work. Does your voice go up a little when you read a question? Do you add feeling when you come to a part that is happy or sad? Remember to use your tone of voice correctly as you read.

- **Pace**: This is the speed at which you read your work. Don't go too fast, but don't go too slow either. Find the correct pace for the piece you are reading.

As you read, make eye contact at times with your audience. This will mean raising your eyes from the paper, but it will add to the reading. Move your gaze to different parts of the audience. You will make them feel you are looking directly at them, and including them in your reading in a more personal way. After reading, listen to comments from the audience, especially if the reading was to try out a piece you needed checked. Be open to their ideas: they might improve your writing in ways you hadn't thought of.

Write a short piece on a topic of your choice. Read it out loud to yourself, then to a friend or group of friends. Use the ideas presented above to make your reading more "alive."

Interviewing

An **interview** is a conversation with another person. Its purpose is to get information. The **interviewer** asks questions, while the **interviewee** (the person being interviewed) answers them.

Here are some ideas to think about if you are the **interviewer**.

- **Prepare for the interview**: Arrange a time and place for the interview. Develop clear questions to ask during the interview. Avoid questions that are answered with *yes* or *no*. Make sure you know something about the person you are interviewing. Gather any materials you need before the interview. If you want to tape-record the interview, ask the interviewee if this is all right.

- **Conducting the interview**: Introduce yourself if necessary. During the interview, be polite. Ask your questions, but don't always rely on your list of questions. Check your notes, looking at the interviewee. Show interest in the subject by giving your own background information where necessary. Let other questions come from information the person gives, if they fit in with your intent for the interview. Give enough time for each answer. End the interview by thanking the interviewee.

Here are some ideas to think about if you are the **interviewee**.

- **Preparing for the interview**: Think about some of the questions that might be asked. Imagine how you might answer them. Be on time for the interview. Relax and try not to be nervous.

- **During the interview**: Listen to each question. Answer only after you have thought about your answer. Speak clearly, with good voice control and proper speech. Answer the questions to the best of your knowledge, but don't say too little or too much. Add points at the end of the interview if the interviewer has given you this opportunity.

Write some ideas here that you would use in an interview if you were the interviewer. Think: What is the interview about? Who is it with? What might I ask? What do I need to know?

_____

_____

_____

_____

_____

_____

_____

_____

Interview Format Sheet

Use this page to organize an interview.

TOPIC: _____   **INTERVIEWER:** _____

INTERVIEWEE: _____   **DATE OF INTERVIEW:** _____

TIME/PLACE OF INTERVIEW: _____

INTERVIEW QUESTIONS:

_____

_____

_____

_____

_____

_____

RESPONSES (point form):

_____

_____

_____

_____

_____

_____

OTHER INFORMATION (e.g., interview tape-recorded; further interview necessary; other people to interview on this topic):

_____

_____

_____

Review/Critique Sheet

Use this page when you review or critique a media production, such as a TV program, movie, or concert.

ITEM REVIEWED: _____

TIME OF REVIEW: _____ **PLACE:** _____

SUMMARY OF ITEM REVIEWED (e.g., TV show, comedy; CD by _____; movie: summarize the main details of the item):

COMMENTS—POSITIVE: _____

_____

_____

_____

_____

COMMENTS—NEGATIVE: _____

_____

_____

_____

_____

COMMENTS—OTHER: _____

_____

_____

_____

_____

SUGGESTIONS FOR IMPROVEMENTS: _____

_____

_____

_____

_____

OVERALL RATING (1: poor; to 5: excellent): _____

Investigative Writing Sheet

Use this page when you wish to investigate an item or idea further.

ITEM/IDEA TO INVESTIGATE: _____

REASONS FOR INVESTIGATING THIS: _____

_____

INFORMATION TO BE RESEARCHED:

_____

_____

_____

REFERENCE SOURCES FOR INFORMATION ON ITEM:

_____

_____

_____

PEOPLE TO CONTACT:

_____

_____

_____

NOTES ON INFORMATION GATHERED:

_____

_____

_____

_____

FORMAT FOR PRESENTING INFORMATION (e.g., report, videotape, speech)**:**

_____

AUDIENCE: _____

Unit 6

Preparing for Tests in Reading and Writing

Introduction

Welcome to "Preparing for Tests in Reading and Writing." This section of *LanguageWorks 9* will help you understand **why** you read and write, and **what** you read and write. You will be asked to think about your own personal views on reading and writing. You will also get a chance to assess and refine your skills in these two areas.

This section is set up in the following way:

- Reading and Writing
  - Why You Read
  - What You Read
  - Why You Write
  - What You Write
  - What to Look for When You Read and Write
- How to Respond to Test Questions
- Sample Reading Tasks
- Sample Writing Tasks

Let's go, then, to the **why** and **what** of reading and writing.

Reading and Writing

Why You Read

Why do people read? Usually, we read for two basic reasons:

• for pleasure;

• for information.

Reading for pleasure can be entertaining, such as when you read a favourite short story or an article in a magazine. **Reading for information** can be necessary and important, such as when you read a textbook, a Web site page, or directions on a map. Each type of reading has its own use. As a reader, you do both types every day.

Write down why you read. Think about all of the times you read, and give reasons why you do so. If convenient, discuss what you have written with a partner or in a group.

_____

_____

_____

_____

_____

_____

_____

_____

_____

_____

What You Read

Now that you've thought about and perhaps discussed **why** you read, think about **what** you read. This can include reading you do in and out of school, for pleasure, and for information. Include any type of reading, no matter how unimportant it may seem to you. This might include TV listings (an informational type of reading), menus, novels, song lyrics, and anything that you read quickly or over a period of time.

Write down what you read. Include as many types of reading material as possible and give reasons why you read them. If convenient, discuss what you have written with a partner or in a group.

_____

_____

_____

_____

_____

_____

_____

_____

_____

Before you leave the **why** and **what** of reading, think about what you like to read the most and what you like to read the least. Write down your ideas in the following chart giving reasons. If convenient, discuss what you have written with a partner or in a group.

What I like to read the most, and why	What I like to read the least, and why

Why You Write

People write to put ideas down on paper so that they can be shared with others. As with reading, we write for two basic reasons:

- for pleasure;

- to share information.

Writing for pleasure can include creating a short story, a play, or a poem. **Writing to share information** can include creating a "how to" manual, an advertisement, a set of directions, or a school assignment. Each type of writing has its own use.

Write down why you write. Think of all the times you write and give reasons why you do so. If convenient, discuss what you have written with a partner or in a group.

_____

_____

_____

_____

_____

_____

_____

_____

_____

_____

_____

What You Write

Now that you've thought about **why** you write, think about **what** you write. This can include writing you do in and out of school, for pleasure, and for information. Include any type of writing you do, no matter how unimportant it may seem to you. This might include writing assignments for school, writing an e-mail to a friend, writing a shopping list for a trip, writing a story or a poem.

Write down what you write. Include as many things that you write, and give reasons why you write them. If convenient, discuss what you have written with a partner or in a group.

_____

_____

_____

_____

_____

_____

_____

_____

_____

Before you leave the **why** and **what** of writing, think about what you like to write the most and what you like to write the least. Write down your ideas in the following chart, including reasons. If convenient, discuss what you write down with a partner or in a group.

What I like to write the most, and why	What I like to write the least, and why

What to Look for When You Read and Write

When you read and write, you do so with a **purpose** in mind. For example, you read a TV listing to see what is on a particular channel at a certain time. If you write an e-mail to someone, the reason can be as simple as saying "Hi!" to a friend, or it can be more complicated such as asking a company for more information about a product. It helps if you know your reasons for reading and writing before starting the task. Here are some ideas that might help you.

Reading

Look for these things when you read a selection:

- a main idea—what is it about?

- real or fictional people—are there any? who are they? what do they say? what do they do?

- setting—where and when does the story take place?

- information—what are the important facts and figures?

- key words—are any words **boldfaced**, underlined, or *italicized*?

- grammar, punctuation, capitalization, and spelling—how are they used to help you understand?

- paragraphs—how are they used to help you understand how the main idea is developed?

- closing or ending—does this help to conclude the selection completely and properly?

Writing

Think about these things when you write:

- main idea—do you know what you want to say about a topic?

- audience—do you know for whom you're writing?

- organizing and linking ideas—are your ideas organized in a proper sequence, flowing naturally one into the other?

- sentence and paragraph structure—have you developed your main idea with supporting details in proper sentences?

- characteristics of the form of writing—do you understand the form that you've chosen to write in (e.g., a note, a summary, a short report)?

- grammar, punctuation, capitalization, and spelling—have you used these correctly to help your reader understand what you want to say?

Write down some things you need to think about in your own reading and writing. You can include ideas from the lists above as they relate to you. If convenient, discuss what you have written with a partner or in a group.

_____

_____

_____

_____

_____

_____

How to Respond to Test Questions

Test questions on reading and writing skills ask you to respond by giving answers or doing something (such as writing a sentence or paragraph). Let's look at some ideas that might help you as you respond to test questions. First let's consider reading.

Answering test questions about reading

Read the following selection carefully.

Without Warning

The village sat quietly that morning. The volcano, long quiet, gave little indication of the disaster to follow. The villagers had lived with their inactive neighbour for so long, they didn't give a second thought when the first rumblings echoed throughout the streets. No one believed what was about to happen. It wasn't possible, they thought, and most ignored the early warnings of the destruction to come.

Suddenly, three hours after the first deep sound came the explosion—a blast that shook every building in the village, blew out windows, and crashed through the hearts of the now frightened population. Frantic, they scurried into cars, ran from house to house,

warning whomever they met, then started fleeing as the ash spewed into the sky, blotting out the sun. A second blast and a scalding mass of lava shot up into the air, fanning out in every direction, burning trees and wooden structures wherever it landed. In very little time, the volcano had levelled most of the outskirts of the village, and was sending its molten troops in to finish the rest.

Less than an hour after the mountain had fired the first salvo, all of the villagers had reached safety far from the outskirts of their hamlet. Many wept as they watched, defenceless, the destruction of their homes, the ending of their livelihoods. Things would never be the same again, now that the mountain had spoken.

Now that you have read the selection, look at the questions that follow. They are similar to the types of questions that could be asked about reading a selection such as "Without Warning."

Answering multiple-choice questions

1. This story is mainly about
   A   a mountain
   Ⓑ   a volcanic eruption
   C   people in a village
   D   lava and volcanic ash

The key words in the introduction to the four choices here are **story** and **mainly about**. The correct answer here is B. As you read through all of the choices, notice that each has something to do with the story, but only B states what the whole story is **mainly about**.

2. Why did the villagers ignore the early warnings from the volcano?
   A   The mountain was their friend.
   B   They were at work.
   C   They didn't hear the sounds.
   Ⓓ   They didn't believe the volcano would erupt.

The key words in the introductory question to the four choices here are **why, villagers, ignore,** and **early warnings**. The correct answer here is D. If you read the other three choices carefully, you'll see that none of them is based on anything that is actually stated in the story.

Note also that the key words **early warnings** appears in the first paragraph, which is where the answer to the question can be found. Choosing D shows an understanding of the connection of information stated in the story and the statement, "No one believed what was about to happen."

Tips!

When answering a multiple-choice question
- identify key words in the introduction to the choices provided
- consider every choice carefully
- eliminate choices that are obviously incorrect, ones that are not supported by information given in the selection
- consider again all choices that *might* be correct
- select the choice that *is* correct, the one that is supported by information that is actually given in the selection

---

Answering questions in a single word, phrase, statement, or list

3. What are the "molten troops" that the author describes in the second paragraph?

   Here is a sample answer:
   The "molten troops" are molten lava coming from the volcano.

The key words in the question here are **what, molten troops,** and **second paragraph. What** helps you identify that this is a short-answer question requiring an answer in a single word, phrase, statement, or list without any explanation. **Molten troops** helps you focus on a specific descriptive detail in the selection. **Second paragraph** helps you focus quickly on a specific paragraph for help with the answer.

The sample answer here correctly makes the connection between lava and the descriptive picture of troops on the move.

Answering questions with an explanation

4. Why would the villagers' lives "never be the same again"?

   Here is a sample answer:
   The villagers' lives would be changed because the volcano's eruption had destroyed their homes and businesses. They would have to rebuild or move away.

The key words in the question here are **why, lives, never,** and **same. Why** tells you that an explanation is required in the answer. **Lives** ties the explanation to the villagers. **Never** and **same** are within quotes, which means that they are words taken directly from the selection, helping you focus on a specific section or paragraph.

This sample answer shows an understanding of **inference**, or the ability to conclude what may happen based on the details provided. In this story, a volcano erupts, destroying a village. The answer correctly infers that the villagers may have to rebuild or move away. A short answer that includes an explanation usually requires two or three short sentences.

5. What do you think the villagers should do after the volcano has stopped erupting?

   Here is a sample answer:
   The villagers should move away to another place. The volcano would have destroyed their homes and the surrounding land so they could not live there. It would also be a good idea to leave the area because the volcano could erupt again, making it too dangerous to live there anymore.

The key words in the question here are **what do you think** and **should do**. Both sets of words are asking you to express an opinion along with an explanation. The sample answer shows an understanding of **inference** and the ability to **extrapolate**, that is, to suggest a possible outcome based on the information provided in the story. It shows that the reader understands the main idea and supporting ideas in the story and uses them to suggest a possible "next step."

Answering test questions related to writing

Now, let's take a look at answering questions or following instructions that require you to do more lengthy writing. More lengthy writing can mean:

- writing a single paragraph

- writing a series of three or four connected paragraphs

The task required in such writing can be to:

- write a single-paragraph summary of a passage provided for you

- write a single paragraph based on information provided for you

- write a series of connected paragraphs in which you support an opinion

- write a series of connected paragraphs in which you provide a short report

Writing a single paragraph

When you are asked to write a single paragraph, remember these points:

- the paragraph should be about one **topic** or thought;

- the paragraph should have a clear **topic sentence**, a sentence that lets the reader know what the topic or thought in the paragraph is;

- the paragraph should have three or four **sentences that support** the topic or thought presented in the topic sentence;

- the paragraph should have a **concluding sentence**, a sentence that restates the topic in different words than those of the topic sentence;

- the paragraph should use **correct grammar**, **punctuation**, **capitalization**, and **spelling** to help your reader understand what you want to say.

Writing a single-paragraph summary

Suppose this test question on writing was given to you: "Write a one-paragraph summary of the selection 'Without Warning.'" To do this, you would have to know what the story is about, and be able to summarize, or retell it in a few short sentences.

Here is a sample answer:

(1) The village sat next to the volcano, but the villagers ignored its rumblings. (2) Suddenly, it erupted. (3) The villagers fled their homes and businesses. (4) Everyone got out safely

and they watched from a distance as the molten lava destroyed their village and their livelihoods.

The writer of this summary paragraph has restated what was said in the story without retelling everything in the story. The writer provides only the important information. A summary should just give the main details of a selection, not **every** detail. Note how the writer summarizes the first paragraph of the selection in sentence 1, the longer second paragraph of the selection in sentences 2 and 3, and the final paragraph of the selection in sentence 4.

Tips!

When writing a single-paragraph summary of a selection
- for each paragraph of the selection, identify the topic sentence that states the topic of the paragraph
- re-state the topic in your own words in a sentence
- use the structure of the selection to help you organize your summary: sequence your sentences according to what's at the beginning of the selection, what is in the middle, and what's at the end

---

Note also that the writer of the sample answer is aware of the points made earlier about writing a single paragraph:

- the paragraph is about one **topic**—the eruption of the volcano

- the paragraph has a clear **topic sentence**—sentence 2, "Suddenly, it erupted."

- the sentences in the paragraph **support** the topic stated in the topic sentence

- the paragraph uses **correct grammar**, **punctuation**, **capitalization**, and **spelling** to help the reader understand what the writer wants to say

Writing a single paragraph based on instructions

Now, suppose this test question was given to you: "Write a single paragraph describing a room, outdoor setting, or object that is familiar to you."

Here is a sample answer:
(1) The room I am most familiar with is my bedroom. (2) It contains a single bed. (3) It also has a chest of drawers with four drawers, a built-in closet, and a window that looks out onto the street. (4) The walls of my bedroom are painted blue, and there is a small red rug on the floor just in front of the closet. (5) All these things make my bedroom a comfortable place to be.

The key words in the instructions here are **single paragraph, room, outdoor setting, object,** and **familiar**. **Single paragraph** tells you, of course, how long your answer should be and that it must be structured as a proper paragraph with a topic sentence and supporting sentences. You are also instructed to choose one of three possible topics (**room, outdoor setting,** or **object**). The topic must also be one that is **familiar** to you, that is, you must know it well enough to provide a realistic description.

In the sample answer, the writer identifies the topic in sentence 1: "my bedroom." The writer then provides descriptive information about the room in sentences 2–4, and provides a concluding sentence (5), in which the topic is restated.

Tips!

When writing a single paragraph based on information provided to you
- identify the key words in the information provided
- note any *qualifying* words: for example, the words *or* and *one of* in the instructions usually mean that you have to choose a topic; adjectives may further limit what you should focus on (if you chose to write about a familiar setting above, for instance, you should write a paragraph about an *outdoor* setting)
- write a clear topic sentence
- write sentences that support the topic sentence
- write a *concluding sentence*, a sentence that restates the topic in different words than those of the topic sentence
- write sentences that use correct grammar, punctuation, capitalization, and spelling to help your reader understand what you want to say

---

Writing a series of connected paragraphs

When you are asked to write a series of connected paragraphs, remember these points:

- the whole series must be about **one main idea**;

- each paragraph should contain one **aspect** or **thought** about the main idea;

- each paragraph should have a clear **topic sentence**, a sentence that lets the reader know what the topic or thought in the paragraph is;

- each paragraph should have three or four **sentences that support** the topic or thought given in the topic sentence;

- the paragraphs should be organized in a proper sequence, flowing naturally one into the other;

- you should understand the **characteristics** of the form you've chosen to write in (e.g., a note, a summary, a short report); and

- **grammar**, **punctuation**, **capitalization**, and **spelling** should be used correctly to help your reader understand what you want to say

Writing a short report

Now, suppose this test question were given to you: Write a short report of three or four connected paragraphs on a news event that includes the following basic details:

- yesterday
- late morning
- figure dressed in bright orange jumpsuit
- 30-storey downtown building

- scales the building
- crowd gathers
- police and fire services arrive
- publicity stunt

Feel free to make up further details for the news report as long as they are related to the ones above.

Here is a sample answer:

Downtown traffic came to a halt just before noon yesterday in front of the Metro Building as crowds gathered to look up at a figure scaling the 30-storey structure. The figure, dressed in a bright orange jumpsuit, was nearly halfway down the side of the building by the time the police and fire services arrived on the scene.

As the figure—later identified as Monica Milo, a part-time acrobat—made her way down the shiny glass side of the building, she waved to the crowd below and showered them with leaflets advertising an upcoming performance of the Rave Rats at the City Club. The crowd waved back and applauded her performance.

When Ms. Milo touched earth, she received a further round of applause. Cameras flashed as she was taken away by the police to be charged for her entertaining and mischievous act.

Note how the writer builds on the details provided in the instructions to create a vivid news report of the event. The writer both fills out the details provided and adds related new details, as called for in the instructions. Note also the details describing the event relate to the W5H of a news report: **who**, **what**, **when**, **where**, **why**, and **how**.

Here are examples of the writer filling out some of the details provided:

- **crowd gathers**: traffic comes to a halt, crowd looks up, crowd waves and applauds
- **figure dressed in orange jumpsuit**: a woman named Monica Milo, part-time acrobat
- **publicity stunt**: advertising Rave Rats performance at the City Club

---

Tips!

When writing a series of connected paragraphs in which you provide a short report based on details provided
- make sure you visualize or imagine the event from the details provided
- make sure you include all the details provided, making them more specific and vivid by filling them out
- make sure your news report covers the W5H of the event: *who, what, when, where, why,* and *how;* present these details in a factual, straightforward way
- make sure that you use grammar, punctuation, capitalization, and spelling correctly to help your reader understand what you want to say

---

Writing a series of paragraphs to support an opinion

Now, suppose this test question were given to you: Write a series of three or four connected paragraphs in which you express and support an opinion about either (a) sports as a business, or (b) violence on television.

Here is a sample answer:

We spend many hours looking at television. But how many of us stop to think about the violence that we see on the screen and the problems it is creating in our society? I think that there are two main problems: the attitude toward violence that we learn from television, and what we don't see because of all of the violence.

The main reason I think this way is because I believe that repeated graphic violence provides young people with dangerous models of behaviour. It can make them think that harming others is exciting and lots of fun. This is clearly not a good message to be sending to young people. There is already too much violence in the real world.

The other reason I think this way is because the great quantity of violence on screen leaves less room for more important subjects to be shown. For example, I would like to see more on television about technology and how it is changing our world. I am not talking just about the hype of cell phones and the Internet but about the pros and cons of such technology: What's good about it? What's bad?

I think, then, that if there is less violence on television, it will help to encourage better attitudes in young people and allow more airtime for more important subjects.

The key words in the instructions here are **series of three or four connected paragraphs** and **express and support an opinion**. The instructions also offer the choice of one of two topics, and the sample answer is in response to the second of the choices, violence on television. **Series of three or four connected paragraphs** tells you how long your answer should be and, in general terms, how it is to be structured. **Express and support an opinion** tells you that you must clearly state an opinion, or point of view about the topic, and that you must back up what you say.

In the sample answer, the writer clearly states an **opinion** in the first paragraph. In the second paragraph, the writer provides a main **reason** for having this opinion, and then **supports** this reason. In the second paragraph, the writer states a second, less important reason and supports this reason also. In the last paragraph, the writer provides a brief **summary** of the reasons stated.

Tips!

When writing a series of connected paragraphs in which you support an opinion
- identify the key words in the information provided
- clearly express your opinion, or point of view, on the topic in the first sentence of the first paragraph
- in general terms, state the reasons for your opinion in the first paragraph; two or three reasons are enough
- explain each of your reasons in a well-developed paragraph (topic sentence and supporting sentences)
- structure your series of paragraphs logically, moving from your most important reason to your least important reason, or vice versa
- make sure that you use grammar, punctuation, capitalization, and spelling correctly to help your reader understand what you want to say

---

Advertisement

Adventure!

It's the thrill of the unknown, and the quest for a thrill.

We seek it out. We want it. We *crave* it.

For some, it's a trip in a raft down a white-water canyon,
with spray from the rapids

crashing against the side of the boat.
For others, it's hang gliding off the edge of a cliff,
overlooking a cityscape below.

For the rest of us, it's the **first bite** and we're in a hot-air balloon over open
countryside,

dodging trees and seagulls as we aim for the coast.

The **second bite** and we're skiing
down a monster trail that whips around a mountainside,
careening past rocky outcroppings and huge trees.

The **final bite** and we explore the outer reaches of space at
the speed of light, shifting into hyperspace on a journey
to the edge of the Universe.

Adventure!

With its mixture of nougat and almonds

in a rich chocolate covering,

a fusion of flavours bursting in your mouth

with every bite,

you'll know the thrill,

and you'll crave it daily.

Seek it out.

Your *Adventure* begins.

Advertisement: *Adventure!*

1. What product is this advertisement selling? Circle the correct answer.

   A   a new sandwich
   B   a skiing holiday
   C   a chocolate bar
   D   a trip to a white-water resort

2. What does the advertisement say we feel about adventure?

   _____

3. Summarize what happens, according to the advertisement, as we take bites of the product.

   _____

   _____

4. One of the lines states "...a fusion of flavours bursting in your mouth..." What does this mean?

   _____

   _____

5. This advertisement compares adventurous activities to eating a new food product. Do you think that this comparison is effective? Give reasons for your answer.

   _____

   _____

6. Would the copy (text) in this advertisement make you want to try the product? Give reasons for your answer.

   _____

   _____

   _____

   _____

   _____

   _____

How a Cell Phone Works

One of the most interesting things about a cell phone is that it is really a radio—an extremely sophisticated radio, but a radio nonetheless. A good way to understand the sophistication of a cell phone is to compare it to a CB radio or a walkie-talkie. A CB radio is a **simplex** device. That is, two people communicating on a CB radio use the same **frequency** so only one person can talk at a time. A cell phone is a **duplex** device, so it uses one frequency for talking and a second, separate frequency for listening. A CB radio has 40 channels. A cell phone can communicate on 1664 channels. Cell phones also operate within cells and they can switch cells as they move around. Cells give cell phones incredible range. A walkie-talkie can transmit perhaps a kilometre and a half. A CB radio, because it has much higher power, can transmit perhaps eight kilometres. Someone using a cell phone, on the other hand, can drive clear across a city and maintain a conversation the entire time. Cells are what give a cell phone its incredible range.

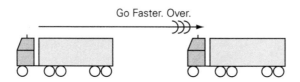

In **simplex radio** (e.g., CB radios), both transmitters use the same frequency. Only one party can talk at a time.

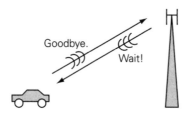

In **duplex radio**, the two transmitters use different frequencies, so both parties can talk at the same time. Cell phones are duplex.

How-it-works article: *How a Cell Phone Works*

1. A cell phone is really a

    A   small television
    B   sophisticated computer device
    C   radio
    D   walkie-talkie

2. Which device has more channels, a CB radio or a cell phone?_____

3. What is the difference between a **simplex** device and a **duplex** device?

    _____

    _____

    _____

4. Why do cell phones have larger transmission ranges than CB radios and walkie-talkies?

    _____

    _____

    _____

5. What do you think are some of the advantages to owning a cell phone?

    _____

    _____

    _____

6. Do you think there are any disadvantages to owning a cell phone? Explain your answer.

    _____

    _____

    _____

    _____

    _____

    _____

Basic Cell Phone

Making a call

1) Extend the phone's antenna fully.

2) Enter the **area code** and **phone number**, then press **SEND**. If you make a mistake, press **CLR** to erase digits one by one. Press and hold **CLR** to clear the whole display.

A phone symbol appears on the display. The call is connected when the phone number disappears from the display and **CALL** appears.

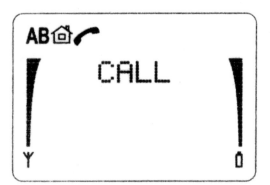

For international calls, you can enter a '+' at the beginning of a number by pressing ******. Then enter the number, then press **SEND**. The '+' expands to the international dialing code prefix.

NO SERVICE appears and the phone beeps if you try to make a call when your phone is outside the cellular service area.

CALL NOT ALLOWED appears if you try to make a call that is restricted or if the phone is locked.

If you receive a call when you're trying to make a call, the incoming call comes through and the outgoing call is cancelled.

Ending a call

Press **End.**

Note: If you press and hold **END**, you'll activate Keyguard.

Keyguard locks the Keypad to prevent accidental use when the phone is stored in a pocket or handbag. To deactivate Keyguard, press **MENU**, then *.

Instructions: *Basic Cell Phone*

1. In making a call, the first step is to

   A extend the base of the phone
   B extend the antenna
   C extend the battery pack
   D extend the call display

2. When do the words CALL NOT ALLOWED appear?

   _____

   _____

3. What happens if you receive a call while trying to make a call?

   _____

   _____

4. After dialing, how do you start a call? How do you end a call?

   _____

   _____

5. How do you know if you are outside the service area?

   _____

   _____

6. Do you think instructions are important to the cell-phone buyer? Explain your answer.

   _____

   _____

   _____

The Canoe

No technology is more associated with Canada than the birch-bark canoe. The First Nations of the Eastern woodlands developed the craft as a precision-built vessel that was both functional and a work of art.

The skills required to build a canoe were numerous, and there were many problems to overcome. Canoe builders needed to know how to harvest bark; prepare pitch; fashion tools; fell trees; split cedar for gunwales, sheathing, and ribbing; bend wood with hot water; lace joins; caulk seams; and etch designs; among various other skills.

Wooden gunwales ran along the top sides of the canoe, and on the inside thinly cut boards were held in place against the birch bark by cedar ribs. All of this intricate woodwork was neatly finished using hand-made stone tools. The bending of the slender cedar ribs after they were soaked in hot water was one of the most delicate operations, requiring great skill and patience.

The skill of canoe building was passed from one generation to the next over centuries. European settlement, however, virtually destroyed this technology of thousands of years. Birch groves dwindled as settlers cleared the forests for farming. As the First Nations moved onto reserves, traditional lifestyles, including the use of canoes, were restricted. Furthermore, the settlers began mass-producing canvas canoes. Canoe-building technology was kept alive by only a handful of Aboriginal artisans.

History textbook information: *The Canoe*

1. Which First Nations people developed the canoe as a precision-built vessel?

   A   Iroquoian Nations
   B   Plains Nations
   C   Eastern woodlands Nations
   D   Northwest Coast Nations

2. Circle three skills canoe builders needed to know.

   A   prepare pitch
   B   use nails
   C   fell trees
   D   trade for tools
   E   harvest bark
   F   talk with neighbours

3. According to the article, European settlement destroyed birch bark canoe-building technology. How did this happen?

   _____

   _____

   _____

4. Was the canoe-building technology kept alive at all? How?

   _____

   _____

   _____

5. In your opinion, which type of canoe is better: a mass-produced one or one made by a First Nations group? Explain your opinion.

   _____

   _____

   _____

   _____

   _____

   _____

Laura Secord's Run

The War of 1812 was the last war fought on Canadian soil. It produced many heroes and tales of bravery. One of the most famous was Laura Secord's run to warn the British troops of a forthcoming American attack.

Born in the United States, Laura had settled in her adult years with her husband in Queenston, Upper Canada. She was intensely loyal to the British crown.

In 1812, the United States declared war on the British colonies of Upper and Lower Canada. Soon, the Americans had a foothold in Upper Canada. On the evening of June 21, 1813, some American officers forced their way into the Secord house and commanded Laura to prepare dinner. After the meal, Laura overheard one of the officers outlining a plan to attack the British troops. Laura was stunned. What could she do to warn the troops? Her husband lay wounded in the bedroom, still recovering from the Battle of Queenston Heights six months earlier.

Suddenly, Laura decided. She would have to make the 30 km trek to the British stronghold and warn Lieutenant FitzGibbon about the planned attack.

Hours passed as Laura hurried through swamp and along escarpment, staying in the thick undergrowth to remain undetected. Finally, she reached a clearing and collapsed from exhaustion. A group of Iroquois surrounded her and helped her to her feet. She explained her mission to them and they took her to FitzGibbon. After getting the details from Laura, FitzGibbon ordered his troops to the ready, and the American offensive was turned back.

Laura Secord's run became part of Canadian folklore, especially after 1860 when the Prince of Wales publicly acknowledged her contribution to the War effort. It's still a mystery why it took so long for Laura to be recognized as a hero. Whatever the reason, Canadians everywhere now know about the woman who risked her life to keep her country loyal to the British crown almost two centuries ago.

History article: *Laura Secord's Run*

1. Laura Secord lived in

   A   Lower Canada
   B   Upper Canada
   C   Eastern Canada
   D   Western Canada

2. Laura was loyal to

   A   the American troops
   B   the Canadian government
   C   the British crown
   D   the President of the United States

3. Why couldn't Laura's husband make the journey to warn the British troops?

   _____

   _____

4. What is a "trek"?

   _____

   _____

5. Who was FitzGibbon?

   _____

   _____

6. Laura's run is described in the article as a part of Canadian folklore. What is "folklore"?

   _____

   _____

   _____

7. What was the result of Laura's run? Explain in your own words.

   _____

   _____

   _____

   _____

   _____

   _____

A Quick History of Rock-and-Roll

For many people, the history of rock-and-roll starts in the early 1950s with the sounds of Bill Haley and the Comets wailing out of radios, or with the even louder wailing of Elvis Presley as he shook, rattled, and rolled his way into the hearts of a generation of screaming fans.

"Not so," say the true historians. They see the roots of rock music going much further back—into African music that was brought to North America on the slave ships that first landed in 1619. African music fused over time with more traditional European musical forms. Late nineteenth century American composers, for example, wrote popular music that owed much of its form and style to the African music that had become such a part of the musical language of the United States.

As the twentieth century dawned, Scott Joplin and his ragtime piano music became the rage. The 1920s and 1930s saw the creation and popularity of dixieland, music that is the direct precursor of modern rock music. They were jumpin', jivin' pieces that got everyone going, and the sound spread right around the world. They led to the big-band sounds of the late 1930s and 1940s: the music of Count Basie, Duke Ellington, Harry James, and Glenn Miller. Soon after came rock-and-roll.

The 1950s saw the rise of a new generation who wanted to dance and hear *their* music. They got it from the likes of Elvis Presley, Buddy Holly, and Richie Valens, singers who proclaimed a new era in music, one that celebrated the young. Rock-and-roll had finally arrived, and the musical world would never be the same again. Even so, the "new" music had evolved from the musical styles of earlier years, going right back to those first slave ships from Africa.

History article: *A Quick History of Rock-and-Roll*

1. The article argues that rock music has its roots in

   A   the 1950s
   B   the 1890s
   C   1619
   D   the nineteenth century

2. Ragtime music was popularized by

   A   Count Basie
   B   late nineteenth century American composers
   C   Dixieland music
   D   Scott Joplin

3. According to the article, what type of music was popular in the 1920s and 1930s?

   _____

   _____

   _____

   _____

   _____

4. Explain why you think the author puts quotation marks around the word **new** in the final paragraph of the article.

   _____

   _____

   _____

   _____

   _____

Global Positioning System (GPS)

Imagine that you wake up one morning and discover that your family vehicle has been stolen. The chances of getting it back are slim, unless it happens to be equipped with a satellite tracking device. This device uses the Global Positioning System (GPS) and can pinpoint the location of your stolen car anywhere on the planet, 24 hours a day. This may sound like science fiction, but GPS technology can be applied in many ways.

An inexpensive GPS tracking device the size of a mobile phone can give users their position in degrees of latitude and longitude. This information can be transmitted by another device to tell other people where you are and how to find you if you are lost. Environmentalists have been using GPS to track wildlife. Shipping companies use GPS technology to monitor the progress of their delivery trucks. Some automobiles have on-board maps that show users their current location. This location is given to a company which, for a fee, provides information about the fastest or most scenic route to a particular destination.

In the future, mobile phones will be GPS-equipped to trace the source of 911 calls. Pet owners will put GPS devices on their dogs and cats to keep track of their whereabouts. Many of the uses of GPS technology have yet to be invented!

Geography textbook information: *Global Positioning System (GPS)*

1. A GPS is a

   A global partitioning system
   B global positioning series
   C global positioning system
   D global practical system

2. A GPS works with what kind of planetary orbiting device?

   _____

3. List three things that can benefit from a GPS.

   _____

   _____

4. Who have been using GPS for years to track wildlife?

   _____

   _____

5. What might be some uses for GPS in the future?

   _____

   _____

   _____

   _____

6. In your opinion, is GPS a useful technology? Explain your answer.

   _____

   _____

   _____

   _____

   _____

   _____

   _____

Glaciers

Glaciers are large, spreading sheets of ice. Glaciers that cover vast areas of land are called **continental glaciers**. Antarctica and Greenland are covered by continental glaciers. Elsewhere in the world, glaciers form high up in mountain ranges where the temperatures are so cold that snow and ice stay frozen all year round. These glaciers, called **valley glaciers**, spread down through the high valleys between the peaks.

When these mountains formed hundreds of millions of years ago, they had tall, sharp peaks like the Rocky Mountains. But, repeated glaciation has worn them down to the rounded hills we see today.

Many lakes in Canada, including the Great Lakes, were formed by the action of glaciers scouring our depressions in the land. The small, round lake in the photo on the right is a **kettle lake**. This type of lake formed when large chunks of ice left behind by a glacier melted away.

As glaciers move, the weight of the ice grinds on the rock that it passes over. Pieces of rock, from tiny fragments to boulders, become embedded in the ice and are carried along. If the climate is cold enough, added snow will cause the glaciers to move forward, covering more and more land. If the climate becomes warmer, glaciers will gradually melt back or retreat, leaving behind the soil, rock, and boulders that they once contained.

Today, we have continental and valley glaciers only in specific areas, but many times over its history, large parts of Earth were covered with glaciers. These were the **Ice Ages**, and much of Canada's geography was shaped by these huge sheets of ice.

Geography textbook and visual information: *Glaciers*

1. Glaciers that cover large areas of land are called

   A icy glaciers
   B continental glaciers
   C valley glaciers
   D mountain glaciers

2. Which kind of glaciers spread down through high valleys between mountain peaks?

   _____

3. If the climate is cold enough, what causes glaciers to move forward?

   _____

4. Glaciers grind the rocks as they pass over the land. What effect might this have on the land as the glaciers move?

   _____

   _____

   _____

5. The article says that much of Canada's geography was shaped by glaciers over its history. What do you think is meant by this?

   _____

   _____

   _____

   _____

   _____

   _____

6. Explain in your own words what you think an Ice Age is.

   _____

   _____

   _____

   _____

   _____

   _____

Population Density

Canada is a very large country with a fairly small population. The relationship between the area and population of a country can be shown using a simple measurement called population density. This can be calculated by dividing the country's population by its area. Let's calculate Canada's population density:

30 600 000 people ÷ 9 922 000 km² = 3.1 people/km² (population density)

This does not mean that there are three people living on each and every square kilometre of Canada. Rather, population density is just a way of making a general comparison of the relationship between the area and the population of a country.

Population densities vary enormously from place to place. The Western Sahara, for example, has 0.8 people/km², while the Falkland Islands has 0.2 people/km². At the other extreme are crowded countries like Singapore (5000 people/km²). If we examine the population densities of countries (Fig. 1-9), we see a smaller, but still significant range of values.

Population Density (People/km²), 1996

Argentina	13	Jamaica	237
Australia	2	Japan	333
Bangladesh	832	Kazakhstan	6
Brazil	19	Nigeria	112
Canada	3	Pakistan	166
China	127	Russia	9
Germany	229	South Africa	36
India	289	Sudan	12
Indonesia	105	United Kingdom	240
		United States	28

Figure 1–9

Geography textbook and tabular information: *Population Density*

1. The population density of a country can be calculated by dividing its population by its

   A   number of provinces
   B   cities
   C   mass
   D   area

2. Population density is a way of making _____ between the area and population of a country.

   A   a general comparison
   B   a large comparison
   C   a small comparison
   D   an exact comparison

3. According to the chart, which country has

   (a) the greatest population density: _____

   (b) the lowest population density: _____

4. According to the table, where does Canada rank in terms of population density?

   _____

5. Does a population density figure mean that every square kilometre of land has a certain number of people? Explain.

   _____

   _____

   _____

6. In your opinion, what benefits are there in knowing the population density of a certain country? Who do you think would find this type of information useful?

   _____

   _____

   _____

   _____

   _____

   _____

   _____

   _____

   _____

Take a Pulse

Do you know someone who acts more dead than alive? Prove they have a pulse! You can feel a pulse every time an artery stretches a tiny bit to allow blood to pass through it. It's easiest to feel a pulse where an artery is just below the skin: the back of the knee, the wrist, the side of the neck.

Put two fingers across your neck. Count the number of pulses you feel in a minute. That's the pulse—it's the same as the number of heartbeats in a minute. It will probably be around 90 beats per minute (an adult's will be around 70 beats per minute).

The pulse speeds up when you get excited or when you exercise. Do some jumping jacks for a few seconds and check your pulse again—it will be about two times as fast as before. Why? Your heart is pumping faster, sending more oxygen to hard-working muscles.

Health information and instructions: *Take a Pulse*

1. What stretches a bit to allow blood to pass through, causing a pulse?

   A   the lungs
   B   an artery
   C   the throat
   D   skin

2. Where are two of the places on the body you can feel a pulse?

   _____

3. To get a pulse reading, you count the number of pulses you feel

   A   in a minute
   B   in a second
   C   in an hour
   D   in twenty seconds

4. Who has a faster pulse: adults or adolescents? Give a reason for your answer.

   _____

   _____

   _____

5. Why does your pulse go faster after exercise?

   _____

   _____

   _____

6. How is the pulse related to heartbeats?

   _____

   _____

   _____

7. In your opinion, is it better to have a faster pulse rate or a slower pulse rate? Explain your answer.

   _____

   _____

   _____

   _____

   _____

   _____

In July 1994, Did We See What Destroyed the Dinosaurs?

Why did the dinosaurs suddenly vanish from Earth 65 million years ago after ruling Earth for 175 million years?

One theory is that a large meteor or comet smashed into the Yucatan Peninsula in Mexico 65 million years ago. The impact was so powerful that huge clouds of dust and debris were sent into Earth's atmosphere, blocking the sun's rays. The reduced heat and light from the sun chilled the climate and destroyed the plants that fed the plant-eating dinosaurs. As their numbers were reduced, the food supply of the meat-eating dinosaurs also disappeared.

Until recently, there was no way to check this theory or to assess what kind of damage such a collision might create. However, in July 1994, something occurred never before seen by humans—a comet collided with the planet Jupiter.

Jupiter is the largest planet in our solar system, with a diameter of approximately 143 000 km compared to Earth's diameter of 12 756 km. The comet, called Shoemaker-Levy 9, was discovered by Canadian scientist David Levy and American scientists Carolyn and Eugene Shoemaker. In 1992, it was pulled in to Jupiter's gravitational field. The comet entered the atmosphere of Jupiter and, on July 16, 1994, the first fragment of the comet smashed into the planet at a speed of 216 000 km/h.

The collision, viewed by the Hubble telescope, revealed an explosion that soared 965 km into the atmosphere. As one scientist exclaimed, "It produced a fireball like that which was predicted. That means that the energy created was equivalent to 200 000 megatonnes of TNT or more!"

Science textbook information: *In July 1994, Did We See What Destroyed the Dinosaurs?*

1. In July 1994, what happened to the planet Jupiter?

    A   It was found to be out of orbit.
    B   It shrunk in size.
    C   It became a failed star.
    D   It was hit by a comet.

2. According to the article, what is one theory as to why the dinosaurs disappeared?

    _____

    _____

    _____

3. According to the article, what did the reduced heat and light from the sun do to Earth's climate?

    _____

    _____

4. According to the article, why did the dinosaurs disappear after the plants were destroyed?

    _____

    _____

5. What evidence does the article give that the collision with Jupiter was very destructive?

    _____

    _____

    _____

6. Comet or asteroid collisions with Earth have often been talked about as being "catastrophic." Explain what this means.

    _____

    _____

    _____

7. In your opinion, how possible is it that a comet may have destroyed the dinosaurs? Explain your answer.

    _____

    _____

    _____

    _____

Mathematics tabular information

The table shows the percentage of households that had certain products in 1988, and the estimated percentages for the year 2000.

Estimated Percentages of Households Using Selected Products				
	% in Canada		% in USA	
	1988	2000	1988	2000
Colour televisions	92	96	93	96
Projection televisions	1	7	3	12
Stereo televisions	10	40	20	50
Video cassette recorders	52	75	56	80
Laptop and personal computers	15	35	17	40
Microwave ovens	54	85	70	90
Compact disc/digital tape equipment	8	75	4	85
Electronic home security systems	5	12	8	15
Three or more telephones	22	45	25	50

Mathematics tabular information: *Estimated Percentages of Households Using Selected Products*

1. According to the table, which product appears in the most households?

    A   Video cassette recorders
    B   Microwave ovens
    C   Colour televisions
    D   Compact disc/digital tape equipment

    _____

2. Which two countries are used for the survey?

    _____

3. Which product is estimated to have the largest percentage change in use from 1988 to 2000 in Canada?

    _____

4. Which product is estimated to have the least percentage change in use from 1988 to 2000 in Canada?

    _____

5. Which products from the table do you feel are the most important to have in the home? Which products from the table are not as necessary to have in the home? Give reasons for your answers.

    _____

    _____

    _____

    _____

    _____

    _____

6. Beyond the year 2000, which products from the table do you feel will have the greatest growth in numbers of households using them? Explain your answer.

    _____

    _____

    _____

    _____

    _____

The Art of Knowing Better

by Drew Hayden Taylor

The birds were quiet now. The last call of the crow and cry of the robin had disappeared with the setting sun. I could tell that the wind, which had died down during the early part of the evening, was picking up once more, rustling the trees and making the smaller ones bow down to the moon. Another evening in Otter Lake.

Outside my room, the summer insects buzzed and crawled across the window screen, trying to get at the light that burned above me. I turned it off. I wanted the quiet of this summer night, as I listened to the village wind down. Another day to be knocked off the calendar. The universal rituals that end all days around the world vary little, even in this small Ojibway community. Everything was finishing as it normally did.

Fictional description: *The Art of Knowing Better*

1. This selection is set

   A   at dawn
   B   mid-morning
   C   at sunset
   D   at night

2. List three sounds that the narrator hears.

   _____

   _____

3. What do you think the narrator means by "universal rituals"?

   _____

   _____

4. Choose one sound or image from the selection and explain why you think it is effective.

   _____

   _____

   _____

   _____

5. What single adjective would you use to describe the mood of this selection? Explain why.

   _____

   _____

   _____

   _____

The Visitation

by Fernando Sorrentino

In 1965, when I was 23, I was training as a teacher of Spanish language and literature. Very early one morning at the beginning of spring I was studying in my room in our fifth-floor flat in the only apartment building on the block.

Feeling just a bit lazy, every now and again I let my eyes stray beyond the window. I could see the street and, on the opposite side, old Don Cesáreo's well-kept garden. His house stood on the corner of a site that formed an irregular pentagon.

Next to Don Cesáreo's was a beautiful house belonging to the Bernasconis, a wonderful family who were always doing good and kindly things. They had three daughters, and I was in love with Adriana, the eldest. That was why from time to time I glanced at the opposite side of the street—more out of a sentimental habit than because I expected to see her at such an early hour.

As usual, Don Cesáreo was tending and watering his beloved garden, which was divided from the street by a low iron fence and three stone steps.

The street was so deserted that my attention was forcibly drawn to a man who appeared on the next block, heading our way on the same side as the houses of Don Cesáreo and the Bernasconis. How could I help but notice this man? He was a beggar or a tramp, a scarecrow draped in shreds and patches.

Fictional narrative: *The Visitation*

1. What was the author training to be in 1965?

   A   a gardener
   B   a teacher of Spanish language
   C   a teacher of Spanish language and literature
   D   a building superintendent

2. What was the narrator doing when he sat by the window early one morning in spring?

   _____

   _____

3. What are some things the narrator could see from the window?

   _____

   _____

   _____

   _____

4. Why is the author particularly interested in the Bernasconis' house?

   _____

   _____

5. The narrator had his attention "...forcibly drawn...." What does this mean?

   _____

   _____

6. The narrator states, "How could I help but notice this man?" Why do you think he says this?

   _____

   _____

   _____

7. What do you think might happen next in the story? Explain your answer.

   _____

   _____

   _____

   _____

   _____

   _____

Fictional narrative

A Hundred Bucks of Happy

by Susan Beth Pfeffer

I found it on the corner of Maple and Grove streets. That isn't the way I usually walk home from school, but that day I had gotten lost in thought and forgotten to turn at Oak, which saves me a half block. Which only goes to prove that daydreaming can be cost-effective.

Anyway, there it was, not exactly glistening in the sunlight, because dollar bills don't glisten. I knew it was a bill of some sort, because it had that well-used green look to it, but I assumed that it was a five, or maybe if my luck were extraordinary, a ten. Whatever it was, I was going to be happy to have it, so I bent down fast, to make sure I got it before anybody else walking down Grove or Maple could find it. It's a well-walked intersection.

I bent down, scooped the money up and started walking away fast, with that heartbeating sensation of having done something exciting and wrong, even though as far as I know, there's no crime in finding money on the street. I've read about people who do that for a hobby, jog with their heads down, collecting the nickels and dimes they find as they run. Whatever this was, it wasn't a dime, and I didn't feel like taking any chances. So I bent, swooped, and increased my pace until by the time I reached Elm I was half running. Not that anybody cared. The rest of the world kept on walking toward whatever their lives were propelling them to. The money was as much mine as if it had been left to me by some munificent great aunt.

I was three doors away from my house before I took the bill out of my jacket pocket, to check its denomination. As I did, I noticed there was a hole in my pocket and the money had slipped into the lining. It took a bit of searching before I found it, but eventually my fingers made contact, and I found what I was looking for.

It was a hundred-dollar bill.

Fictional narrative: *A Hundred Bucks of Happy*

1. At the beginning of the story, the narrator is at the corner of Maple and Oak streets because

    A   the narrator is lost
    B   the narrator is daydreaming
    C   the narrator usually goes this way on the way home from school
    D   the narrator is taking a short cut on the way home from school

2. The narrator describes a great aunt as "munificent"? Which of the following best defines this word?

    A   kind
    B   generous
    C   thoughtful
    D   considerate

3. The narrator refers to people who collect nickels and dimes as they jog. Why do you think the narrator makes this reference?

    _____

    _____

    _____

    _____

4. Why do you think the narrator begins walking faster as the story develops?

    _____

    _____

    _____

    _____

5. What do you think the narrator will do next? Explain your reasons.

    _____

    _____

    _____

    _____

Catch

by Sarah Ellis

"It's a rite of passage," said my aunt Darlene.

We were sitting in an ice-cream parlour celebrating the fact that I had just passed my driving test.

Darlene raised her Coke float. "Welcome to the adult world. May all your parallel parks be perfect."

I held up a spoonful of hot fudge sundae. "To a good teacher." Darlene was a good teacher, patient and funny. She had taken over my driving instruction from Dad, who got so nervous with me at the wheel that he burped all the time.

"She'll talk your ear off," Dad warned.

She did, a continuous commentary insulting the behaviour of other drivers. It made my nervousness dissolve. I'll take talking over burping any time.

"We just don't have enough rituals for these occasions," said Darlene. "We really need something in this culture—a chant or a dance or some libation to the goddess of the road."

"Ice cream is just fine," I said.

"These passages of our lives are what connect us to the great cycles of existence…"

Fictional dialogue: *Catch*

1. Aunt Darlene taught the narrator

   A how to drive
   B how to be patient
   C how to burp
   D how to be funny

2. How did the narrator's father show that he was nervous when he took the narrator out for a driving lesson?

   _____

3. What was the father's warning about aunt Darlene?

   _____

4. Aunt Darlene called passing a driving test a "rite of passage." What did she mean by this?

   _____

   _____

5. "We just don't have enough rituals for these occasions," said Darlene. What is a *ritual*? What do you think aunt Darlene means by her statement?

   _____

   _____

   _____

   _____

   _____

6. How would you describe the relationship between the narrator and aunt Darlene? Give reasons for your answer.

   _____

   _____

   _____

   _____

   _____

   _____

Sample Writing Tasks

Paragraph

Write a paragraph of at least five sentences on *one* of the following topics. Before writing, you might want to reread the section on page 144 on writing a paragraph.

    A   Studying for a test
    B   Raising a pet
    C   Finding a lottery ticket
    D   Seeing a favourite movie

_____

_____

_____

_____

_____

_____

_____

_____

Summary

Write a one-paragraph summary of the article "The Canoe" (see page 154). Before writing, you might want to reread the section on pages 143–144 on writing a summary.

_____

_____

_____

_____

_____

_____

_____

Short News Report

Write a short report of three or four connected paragraphs on one of the following news events. Include the basic details provided below for the event you choose. Feel free to make up further details for the news report as long as they are related to the ones provided. Before writing, you might want to reread the section on page 146 on writing a short news report based on details provided.

A "Visit of Well-known Local Personality to School"
   • personality known for service to community
   • invited by students' council
   • part of speakers' series
   • sell-out, appreciative audience

B "Opening of New Community Centre"
   • opened last week
   • much needed centre
   • variety of facilities offered
   • conveniently located

C "Snow Storm Cripples Area"
   • unexpected storm
   • last night
   • roads unusable
   • major damage to trees

_____

_____

_____

_____

_____

_____

_____

_____

_____

_____

_____

_____

Opinion Piece

Write a series of at least four paragraphs that present your opinion on a topic of your choice. Before writing, you might want to reread the section on page 147 on writing a series of connected paragraphs in which you support an opinion.

_____

_____

_____

_____

_____

_____

_____

_____

_____

_____

_____

_____

_____

_____

_____

_____

_____

_____

_____

_____

_____

Credits

p. 150 "How a Cell Phone Works" from How Stuff Works (http://www.howstuffworks.com), by Marshall Brain. HowStuffWorks.com, Inc., 1999; **p. 152** "Basic Cell Phone Instructions" from Nokia Products Ltd.; **p. 154** "The Canoe" from *Atlantic Canada in the Global Community* by James Crewe, Russell McLean, William Butt, Robert Kenyon, Deirdre Kessler, Dennis Minty, and Elma Schemenauer. Copyright © 1998 Breakwater Books Ltd./Prentice Hall Ginn Canada Inc. Reprinted by permission from Breakwater Books Ltd. and Pearson Education Canada; **p. 160** "Global Positioning System" from *Making Connections: Canada's Geography* by Bruce Clark. Copyright © 1999 Prentice Hall Canada. Reprinted by permission from Pearson Education Canada; **p. 162** "Glaciers" from *Science & Technology*, Grade 8 by Kyn Barker, Steve Campbell, Gary Greenland, Douglas Hayhoe, Doug Herridge, Kathy Kubota Zarivnij, Shelah Reading, Lionel Sandner, and Beverley Williams. Copyright © 2000 Addison Wesley Longman Ltd. Reprinted with permission from Pearson Education Canada. Visuals: "Mountains" from Victoria Hurst/First Light, "Kettle Lake," from Ivy Images; **p. 164** "Population Density" from *Making Connections: Canada's Geography* by Bruce Clark. Copyright © 1999 Prentice Hall Canada. Reprinted by permission from Pearson Education Canada; **p. 166** "Take a Pulse" from "Dracula's Dinner," appearing in *SightLines 8* by Alice Barlow-Kedves, Judy Onody, Thora O'Grady, Wendy Mathieu, and Susan Tywoniuk. Copyright © 1999 Prentice Hall Canada. Reprinted with permission from Pearson Education Canada; **p. 168** "In July 1994, Did We See What Destroyed the Dinosaurs?" from *Minds on Math 8* by Robert Alexander, Katie Pallos-Haden, Ron Lancaster, Fred Crouse, David DeCoste, Brendan Kelly, Florence Glanfield, Paul Atkinson, and Jane Forbes. Copyright © 1998 Addison Wesley Longman Ltd. Reprinted with permission from Pearson Education Canada; **p. 170** "Estimated Percentages of Households Using Selected Products" from *Mathematics 9* by Robert Alexander, Barbara J. Canton, Peter J. Harrison, Rob McLeish, Nick Nielsen, and Margaret Sinclaire. Copyright © 1999 Addison Wesley Longman Ltd. Reprinted with permission from Pearson Education Canada; **p. 172** Excerpt from "The Art of Knowing Better" appearing in *Fearless Warriors* by Drew Hayden Taylor. Published by TalonBooks, 1998; **p. 174** "The Visitation" by Fernando Sorrentino, from *Celeste Goes Dancing and Other Stories* edited by Norman Di Giovanni. Published by Constable & Robinson Publishing Ltd. Reprinted by permission; **p. 176** "A Hundred Bucks of Happy" by Susan Beth Pfeffer, from *Visions* by Donald R. Gallo, Editor. Copyright © 1987 by Susan Beth Pfeffer. Used by permission of Dell Publishing, a division of Random House, Inc.; **p. 178** Excerpt from "Catch" appearing in *Back of Beyond*. Copyright © 1996 by Sarah Ellis. First published in Canada by Groundwood Books/Douglas & McIntyre. Reprinted by permission of the publisher.